ADAM AND EVE AFTER THE PILL, REVISITED

MARY EBERSTADT

Adam and Eve after the Pill, Revisited

With a Foreword by Cardinal George Pell

IGNATIUS PRESS   SAN FRANCISCO

Cover photographs from IstockPhoto.com

Cover design by John Herreid

© 2023 by Ignatius Press, San Francisco
All rights reserved
ISBN 978-1-62164-612-9 (HB)
ISBN 978-1-64229-263-3 (eBook)
Library of Congress Control Number 2022938526
Printed in the United States of America ♾

To Kathryn Jean Lopez,
courageous witness and faithful friend

CONTENTS

FOREWORD

In 1868, Matthew Arnold wrote the beautiful poem "Dover Beach" dedicated to two themes, the first of which is the decline of faith. The world has changed mightily since 1868. The British and French Empires are gone; the United States is the only superpower, to be joined by a resurgent and aggressive Middle Kingdom, the People's Republic of China. The two major forces hostile to Christianity, and faith of any sort, Communism and Nazism have both been defeated. Living standards, health and education, travel, longevity, and literacy have improved dramatically. We have nuclear bombs and nuclear power. The centre of the world is now found in the Pacific Ocean, not the Atlantic. How has faith coped?

Those of us in the Anglosphere must acknowledge a new development in Catholic history because most of the best commentators on faith and modern life are now writing in English. One might rightly claim that this simply contin- ues the tradition established by our own Saint John Henry Newman, continued by Chesterton and Belloc, C. S. Lewis, and the Oxford chaplain Monsignor Ronald Knox. Tolkien's marvellous contribution stands in parallel to this, but today, in the English-speaking world, we are blessed with writers whose contributions are essential to identify- ing where the Catholic community is in the marshes and whirlpools of our often frantic prosperity. The Anglophone ascendency is also explained by the fact that the theological giants from continental Europe at the time of the Second

Vatican Council, such as Yves Marie-Joseph Congar, O.P., Karl Rahner, S.J., Hans Urs von Balthasar, Henri de Lubac, S.J., Jean Daniélou, S.J., and Edward Schillebeeckx, O.P., are no longer with us and have not been replaced.

We have George Weigel from the United States, Father Raymond de Souza from Canada, Ross Douthat at the *New York Times*, Rod Dreher with his Benedict option, and perhaps most perceptive of them all, Mary Eberstadt, also from the United States. I have recommended particularly her marvellously titled book *Adam and Eve after the Pill* (2012), which sets out to explain how the invention of the contraceptive pill has produced a revolution in daily life with consequences as important as those which followed the Marxist-Leninist triumph in the Russian Revolution in 1917. This is a large and controversial claim that outlines the challenges we confront.

Now Eberstadt follows that first book with a new one, continuing the argument from the widest possible angle. *Adam and Eve after the Pill, Revisited* looks at the consequences of the sexual revolution in three large arenas: Western societies, politics, and churches. Once more, Eberstadt presents substantial empirical evidence for her central claim: the individual atomization and familial collapse brought on by the revolution have gone on to transform society and politics. They have also wounded the churches from within, at times mortally. This historical fact, Eberstadt argues, should be the caution of first resort as some within the Catholic Church seek to run the same disastrous experiment.

In addition to its chapters, I recommend the epilogue to this new book, entitled "What Are Believers to Do? The Cross amid the Chaos", based on an address Eberstadt gave to the Society of Catholic Social Scientists in 2021. It begins with an insight from an interview Evelyn Waugh gave to a newspaper in 1930, giving reasons for his conversion to Catholicism. He said, "In the present phase of European history, the essential issue is no longer between Catholicism, on one side, and Protestantism, on the other, but between Christianity and chaos."

What struck me was Waugh seeing chaos as the alternative in 1930 and Eberstadt adopting this term to describe our situation today. Eberstadt acknowledges that the chaos Waugh rejected in the 1930s, residing in "war, dislocation, and stupendous carnage", was different from ours. However, many social pillars were still firm, including the battered institution of the family; "a Christian understanding of creation and redemption and meaning still prevailed in the West." Under Pius XI in the 1930s and indeed Pius XII, Catholic teachings remained "coherent and consistent", the main reason for Waugh's conversion, although chaos had started its work in the Protestant churches.

By coincidence, I recently reread the Russian Aleksandr Solzhenitsyn's 1983 Templeton Address, where he warned against the atheist teachers in the Western world teaching their people to hate their own society. Eberstadt is particularly scathing about elite education in the United States, which she sees as "hiding in a postmodern cuckoo's nest for decades". Too many who do not believe in truth "now run institutions charged with discerning it", she claims, observing further that, "if there is no truth, there are no contradictions." In addition to family chaos, psychic chaos, anthropological chaos, and intellectual chaos, she finds her final example of contemporary chaos in the Catholic Church in the Western world, among those who want to transform Catholic teaching and are often hostile toward those who hold and teach the tradition. In the term "proabortion Catholic", she sees as much sense as in the terms "atheist chaplain" and "former man". Here, for her, we have a "signature irrationalism", a demand that we cancel Aristotle and believe "A and not-A at once".

For a cautious prelate like myself, committed to hoping the glass is half full rather than almost empty, these claims are unpalatable. But while I can point to many places where such extreme alternatives do not flourish, I cannot deny the logic of the claims where such forces are in play.

As both of Eberstadt's *Adam and Eve* books affirm, secular modernity causes multiple forms of suffering that we can often ameliorate when we understand their true origins. We also need to remember that Christ was a healer of the blind, the disabled, the sick, and the possessed. We need to bring his healing to others. Eberstadt is quite explicit that this truth has gone unsaid for too long. Secularism is an inferior culture, small of heart, which defines suffering down, so that victims are not acknowledged as victims but as justified collateral damage. Compare this to the heart of the Lord we see in the Gospels, in his response to the victims of sin and suffering. This is the heart that we must have.

I believe that today's generation of young Christian intellectuals are presented with an unusual opportunity to speak the truth to the void, to give voice to the voiceless, as Eberstadt says here. Change for the better will only occur when many voices present the facts, figures, arguments, and evidence about the human causes and costs of the secularization push. The chaos should be named and shamed, while Christians continue to show that they will not abandon those who have been abandoned, offering them instead healing and friendship and the Good News of the one true God's great love for us.

Cardinal George Pell

INTRODUCTION

In 2012 Ignatius Press published a volume titled *Adam and Eve after the Pill: Paradoxes of the Sexual Revolution*. Its thesis was straightforward: contrary to the secularist, triumphalist view dominant in the Western world since the 1960s, according to which the revolution has been a boon for mankind, evidence has been mounting year by year, decade by decade, on behalf of a contrary assessment.

The alternative verdict is that the gains made by women in the paid marketplace have to be balanced against the concomitant, ongoing disruption of elemental institutions, on a scale never seen before. Evidence abounds that unprecedented sexual consumerism has complicated relations between the sexes more than any other force since Eve took the figurative apple; that the results are documented through the instruments of modern social science, as well as through popular culture and other bellwethers; and that the toll of this experiment has fallen heaviest on the weakest of shoulders—from the unborn sacrificed in its name, to the children and women and men whose lives it continues to scar.

To say that this summation was contrarian is to understate. As was hoped, the book was discussed in depth across religious and religious-friendly media. Its argument was meanwhile ignored in the secular press and nonreligious academia, despite the fact that it required no religious assumptions and despite an open appeal to readers regardless of sectarian leanings. This silence, too, came as no shock.

Most works put out by religious publishing houses are now considered verboten outside those communities, especially any that question secularism's implied monopoly on the common good.

Even so, other fallout came as a surprise—in particular, the emotional reaction of some readers. After all, *Adam and Eve after the Pill* was neither intended nor executed as a volume of self-help. It made no sentimental appeals. Its arguments, though unorthodox in this day and age, were also unexcited; they were served up via cold utensils of data and logic. And although I had tried to avoid boring readers into narcolepsy, I did not, and do not, believe that the book's prose accounted for the force of those responses.

Yet force there was. As the volume made the rounds, first in English and then in other languages, evidence of its unexpected resonance continued to accumulate not only in e-mail, but in the rounds of real life. Often, following a book talk, individuals in the audience would linger and confide hard personal stories of blight, of families and children lost to the revolution's troika: divorce, pornography, abortion.

A few snapshots. In response to one chapter, a man who had lived on the streets, prostituting himself, posted extraordinary commentaries online about how postrevolutionary permissiveness had nearly destroyed him. Another time, after a talk delivered in Texas, a woman said that meditating on today's disarray had encouraged her to have more children. (Her friend affirmed that this was true; they produced photos as proof.) Following a speech in Ohio, in a different year, a young woman came forward to tell of the pain she had suffered as a child from sexual abuse, and her resulting conversion to Christianity.

What to make of such unbidden, raw testimonials, in response to a presentation of facts? Puzzling this out over the years, three conclusions took shape.

The first, and most obvious, was that these stories amounted to inadvertent affirmation of the book's thesis: the post-1960s disorder was indeed generating casualties of all kinds—and their suffering was not being noticed, let alone validated or addressed, by a secularizing culture steeped in denial.

Also clear in hindsight, some readers were galvanized by a different current in the book: the idea that the sexual revolution was open for questioning *at all*. After all, ever since the 1960s, liberationists have anchored their successes to the supposed inevitability of history. The suggestion, offered by *Adam and Eve after the Pill*, that these same changes might *not* be permanent—that they could be subject like any other social phenomena to scrutiny and revision—seemed to some an overdue step forward.

A third conclusion also materialized in retrospect. Like Rosencrantz and Guildenstern, *Adam and Eve after the Pill* had wandered unknowingly into a wider drama. The book's contrarian case implicitly raised a question outside its own parameters: If the secular consensus could whitewash the human damage out there in the name of progress, what other critical fallout might it be missing?

This leads us to the book at hand. *Adam and Eve after the Pill, Revisited* is both a follow-on to the original and a new argument based on the ensuing decade's worth of related research and writing. Like the original, its logic has been worked out more or less methodically in essays and other work, amended and updated as necessary, all united by the same motivation: the desire to understand through empiricism the fruits of the metamorphic seeds planted in the 1960s.

The distinction between the two volumes is simple. *Adam and Eve after the Pill* examined what might be called the *microscopic* effects of the revolution: its fallout on individual men, women, and children, including the transformed moral ecosphere.[1] *Adam and Eve after the Pill, Revisited* widens the aperture to assess the revolution's *macroscopic* fallout: its extensive and compounding effects on society, politics, and Christianity itself.

Chapter 1 bridges the two books by summarizing new material pertinent to the first book's subtitle, "Paradoxes of the Sexual Revolution". It outlines five ways in which the embrace of contraceptive sex turned out to have consequences that were not only unintended, but typically the *opposite* of what revolutionaries had rosily forecast. Instead of lowering rates of abortion, out-of-wedlock births, divorce, and fatherlessness, as was promised, it accelerated all of the above.

As before, proof issues not from philosophy or theology, but from the social sciences and related empirical evidence. To be sure, some deep minds within religious orbits *did* anticipate that the revolution's toll would be steep (most notably in the 1968 papal encyclical, *Humanae Vitae*). Ironically, though, it has fallen to observers more interested in the natural order than in the supernatural to analyze and assemble the supporting facts.

Chapters 2 through 4 reflect on the book's macrocosmic questions, "What Is the Revolution Doing to Society?"

One answer begins in chapter 2, which details a phenomenon now daily strangling open discussion across the West: "the new intolerance" or what has later come to be called "cancel culture". This is "the slow-motion marginalizing and penalizing of believers on the very doorsteps of the churches ... in societies that are the historical

---

[1] So, for example, that book included two chapters on the postrevolutionary "transvaluation of values" which inverted previous taboos—one examining today's ubiquitous pornography, and another the migration of moral poles concerning food and sex.

strongholds of political and religious liberty".[2] This chapter moves beyond the limited focus on free speech to make a wider point: today's intolerance increases human misery via its increasing interference with good works, especially Christian efforts to help the poor.

Chapter 3, "From Revolution to Dogma: The Zealous Faith of Secularism", explains that this new intolerance is no passing nuisance, but a full-blown, quasi-religious, substitute faith for Christianity. Its dogma both derives from, and is designed to protect, the sexual revolution itself. To understand why questions of religious liberty arise so fast and furiously these days, it is critical to grasp this point. Out of secularism has emerged a new creedal system rooted in rejection of the Christian moral code, complete with gnostic founding texts and founders, gnostic equivalents of saints and sacraments, and other sepulchral pantomimes of Christianity itself.

Chapter 4, "Men Are at War with God", looks at the Achilles' heel of this competitor to Christianity: its flawed anthropology. Aleksandr Solzhenitsyn remarked more than once that the twentieth century could be reduced to four words: "Men have forgotten God." The twenty-first century can be distilled in six: "Men are at war with God", specifically over the question of who owns creation.

This paradigm reorders what appear to be isolated social phenomena into a connected whole. Today's obsession with transgenderism, for example, is of a piece with other attempts at derailing the created order, such as abortion and euthanasia. Rage against creation also underlies the destigmatization of nearly all forms of sexual expression (pedophilia excepted, at least for now). Each of these rebellions

---

[2] For a longer analysis of the rise of anti-Christian sentiment and its consequences for religious freedom, see Mary Eberstadt, *It's Dangerous to Believe: Religious Freedom and Its Enemies* (New York: Harper, 2016).

has unfolded uniquely. But all reject the idea that there might be moral limits to human reinvention. Given the evidence presented here about trauma and mental trouble among the young, transgender and otherwise, the refusal to draw authoritative lines around reinvention is not only short-sighted. It is generating novel forms of suffering all its own.

The next part addresses another broad question, "What Is the Revolution Doing to Politics?"

Chapter 5, "Two Nations, Revisited", reviews parts of the record assembled by blue-chip social science. It reflects on a landmark speech delivered in 1997 by James Q. Wilson, former president of the American Political Science Association and one of the most renowned thinkers of his era in the Anglosphere. Borrowing from former Prime Minister Benjamin Disraeli's 1887 image of the "two nations" of the United Kingdom, divided along material lines, Wilson argued that by the end of the twentieth century, the United States has also become "two nations"—this time divided not by material differences, but by an immaterial, yet essential, divide over the family, which now trumps money, social class, and even race as the most reliable predictor of better or worse outcomes.

Chapter 6, "How the Family Gap Undercuts Western Freedom", shows how family combustion has catapulted out of sociology textbooks and onto Main Street. First, the new secularist religion, written increasingly into Western law and mores, cannot help but clash with freedom of religion. Second, endemic postrevolutionary dislocations have also given rise to the signature of the age: identity politics.[3] The decline of the family, combined with the

---

[3] This theme is developed at book length in Mary Eberstadt, *Primal Screams: How the Sexual Revolution Created Identity Politics* (West Conshohocken, PA: Templeton Press, 2018), with commentaries by Rod Dreher, Mark Lilla, and Peter Thiel.

closely related eclipse of organized religion, has left many atomized Western individuals unable to supply an answer to the eternal question, *Who am I?*, by resort to conventional models of family or faith.[4] The result is today's desperate scramble for substitute markers of identity, however ersatz and inferior and however destructive to self and country.

Chapter 7, "The Fury of the Fatherless", applies this theory via an examination of events in the United States in summer 2020, when protests over the death of George Floyd transmogrified into over ten thousand incidents of "unrest" across the country, five hundred of which turned violent. This unparalleled explosion amounts to more proof of the cumulative thesis of part 3: that, as the ending of this chapter summarizes, life without father, Father, and filial piety are not the socially neutral options that contemporary liberalism holds them to be. The sinkhole into which all three have collapsed is now a public hazard.

Part 4 asks one more consequential question: "What Is the Revolution Doing to the Church?"

Chapter 8, "The Doomed Experiment of Christianity Lite", details how Christianity has come apart during the past century because its members have split into two camps: one hoping that the revolution can be accommodated in whole or in part without damaging anything essential about the faith, and another convinced by history that this experiment has been tried over and over and has failed. This chapter traces the undoing of the mainline Protestant churches, including the Anglican Communion, over their chronically unsuccessful attempts to build the Church of "Nice".

---

[4] The relationship between the postrevolutionary fracturing of churches and the concomitant fracturing of the family, which amounts to an alternative theory of Christianity's current decline in the advanced nations, is the subject of another book, Mary Eberstadt, *How the West Really Lost God: A New Theory of Secularization* (West Conshohocken, PA: Templeton Press, 2013).

One result has been death by demographics. Softened dogma became the new Pied Piper, making children vanish from the pews. It further implied that Christians who only stand and wait—or lie in bed on Sunday, watching Netflix—also serve. One more outcome has been doctrinal subversion. First, limited exceptions are made to a rule; next, those exceptions are no longer limited and become the unremarkable norm; finally, that new norm is itself sanctified as theologically acceptable.

In a moment of open talk about official changes to bedrock moral teachings of the Catholic Church, this chapter may be the most cautionary in the book. The persisting notion that mercy and moral norms are somehow at odds is confuted by the evidence. Many children of the revolution are miserable today not because they have too many norms, but too few. The normalization of mores that are making people miserable is not mercy. It risks acquiescence to malady and scants the universal need for redemption

Chapter 9, "What Really Causes Secularization?", turns from doctrinal collapse to sociological reality. It documents problems with conventional accounts of de-Christianization and puts forward an alternative account: the dismantling of so many families has ripped the struts out from under the Church.

The last chapter of this new book, "The Prophetic Power of *Humanae Vitae*", written on the occasion of the encyclical's fiftieth anniversary, reinforces a key claim of both volumes. Fundamental teachings stretching back to the days of the early Church are receiving unintended corroboration in the postrevolutionary age—even as many Catholics and other Christians continue to hope against the ledger that a Church of Nice will someday succeed. The revolution's toxic legacy *itself* amounts to tacit vindication of longstanding teaching concerning sex and marriage—whether or not that vindication is widely understood.

The book's appendix, "The Meaning of *Dobbs*", reflects on the most transformative legal event in the near-half century since *Roe v. Wade* became law: the United States Supreme Court 2022 ruling in *Dobbs v. Jackson Women's Health Organization.*

It is almost impossible to overstate the significance of the court's ruling that, contrary to almost fifty years of misguided jurisprudence, the U.S. Constitution does not confer a "right" to dispose of the unborn—let alone a right to abort at any moment of any pregnancy up until the moment of birth, as advocates for abortion have demanded. In returning the question of *Roe* to the states, the ruling has not only dismantled the recondite legal reasoning that countenanced sixty-three million abortions since 1973. As explained in the appendix, it also raises implicitly a tantalizing prospect: the reexamination of the sexual revolution is no longer a boutique exercise by marginalized religious voices, but an overdue social correction. In other words, *Dobbs* may turn out to be exactly what its detractors fear most: the first step toward rolling back a ruthless, even larger experiment that looks foreordained no more.

Are there alternative readings of the record, according to which the sexual revolution plays a less substantive, more subordinate role in society, politics, and church? Of course there are.

One common rejoinder, for example, is that laments about social dissolution have become endemic. That is true.[5]

---

[5] Liberal intellectual Mark Lilla, for example, observed in his response to my book *Primal Screams* (2019) that "conservatives are addicted to narratives of decline."

But this observation by itself skirts the merits of the argument. Readers concerned with truth should instead ask these questions: *Did the revolution usher in widespread social decline? Or did it not?* The evidence presented in *Adam and Eve after the Pill*, as well as in this current volume, may be unwelcome. But that does not make it less compelling.

Other critics make a different point. Because of internet pornography, some say, sex crimes are down, sexual activity is also diminishing, and society continues to muddle along. In other words, thanks to ubiquitous smut, there is no social problem to see here.[6] This, too, is a nonanswer to the query of what the postliberation era has really wrought. It works only if one turns a cold eye to the dystopic creation of chronically stupefied young men for whom love and romance have become unachievable, thanks to pornography.

And, of course, a third source of reluctance to call things by their rightful names is fear—fear of being ostracized; fear of losing the best seats at the table; fear of surrendering the cool-kid flag, in a time when the failure to wave it will be noticed. So enormous are the revolution's claims on today's lives and loyalties that reflexive denial makes deep emotional sense. But logical sense, again, remains something else.

In sum, critics who object that the sexual revolution is merely epiphenomenal need to contend with the countermanding evidence in both books. This is all the more obligatory as new shoots of revisionist research break through this same stony ground. Such like-minded offerings speak to a growing willingness to face facts. During the years between the first volume and this one, what used to be considered unsayable has become markedly less so.

---

[6] See, for example, Michael Castleman, "Evidence Mounts: More Porn, Less Sexual Assault", *Psychology Today*, January 14, 2016, https://www.psychologytoday.com/us/blog/all-about-sex/201601/evidence-mounts-more-porn-less-sexual-assault.

When *Adam and Eve after the Pill* first appeared a decade ago, its contrarian critique lay well outside mainstream opinion. It still does. But today, it is joined by other countercultural readings of the times. New and diverse critics have come to agree that the status quo demands a closer look.

Within the ranks of traditionalists themselves, books and essays have proliferated during the past decade that challenge the dominant secular narrative.[7] Of particular note was a landmark symposium held on May 31, 2018, in Washington, D.C., titled "The #MeToo Moment: Second Thoughts on the Sexual Revolution". It featured testimony by physicians, attorneys, therapists, and other scholars.[8] Numerous offerings came from women who object to the dehumanized roles in which *women,*

---

[7] See Helen M. Alvare, ed., *Breaking Through: Catholic Women Speak for Themselves* (Huntington, IN: Our Sunday Visitor, 2012); Mary Rice Hasson, *Promise and Challenge: Catholic Women Reflect on Feminism, Complementarity, and the Church* (Huntington, IN: Our Sunday Visitor, 2015); see also Jennifer Roback Morse, *The Sexual State: How Elite Ideologies Are Destroying Lives and Why the Church Was Right All Along* (Gastonia, NC: TAN Books, 2018). For a scholarly examination of the nonliberationist roots of modern feminism and female suffrage, see Erika Bachiochi, *The Rights of Women: Reclaiming a Lost Vision* (Notre Dame, IN: University of Notre Dame Press, 2021).

[8] The symposium was cosponsored by Notre Dame University's Center for Ethics and Culture, the Catholic Women's Forum at the Ethics and Public Policy Center, the Catholic Information Center, and the Archdiocese of Washington. For accounts, see, for example, Susan Brinkdmann, "Women Rethink the Sexual Revolution", *Women of Grace*, June 11, 2018, https://www.womenofgrace.com:8443/blog/?p=64713; Charles C. Camosy, "The #MeToo Moment: Second Thoughts on the Sexual Revolution", *Crux*, June 9, 2018, https://cruxnow.com/interviews/2018/06/the-metoo -moment-second-thoughts-on-the-sexual-revolution; Emma Vinton Restuccia, "Women at Conference Speak Up about #MeToo Movement, Sexual Revolution", *National Catholic Reporter*, June 5, 2018, https://www.ncronline. org/news/people/women-conference-speak-about-metoo-movement-sexual -revolution; and Brandon Showalter, "#MeToo Illuminates Lies of Hedonism: Church Locked in 'Mortal Combat' with Sexual Revolution Scholar", *Christian Post*, June 6, 2018, https://www.christianpost.com/news/metoo-era -illuminates-lies-of-hedonism-church-locked-in-mortal-combat-with-sexual -revolution-scholar.html.

specifically, have been cast by the narrative of liberation.[9] Their analyses have been joined by other commentators who likewise zero in on the epochal transformations since the 1960s.[10]

In a related development, writers from outside religious precincts continue to produce other analyses compatible with that of *Adam and Eve after the Pill*. In the U.K., France, and Germany, three such volumes have broken through to become objects of vigorous discussion.[11] To these examples may be added the abundant literary evidence in the *oeuvre* of French novelist Michelle Houellebecq, whose deadened, desperate postmodern men and women amount to poster children for today's counterrevolutionaries.[12]

---

[9] As theologian Deborah Savage summarizes one main line of thought: "The contraceptive mind-set that governs our culture is an affront to the dignity of woman because it is a declaration that who she is, in her very being, is not wanted." "Reflections on the Revolution", *First Things*, October 2018, https://www.firstthings.com/article/2018/10/reflections-on-the-revolution.

[10] See Scott Yenor, *The Recovery of Family Life: Exposing the Limits of Modern Ideologies* (Waco, TX: Baylor University Press, 2021); Carl Trueman, *The Rise and Triumph of the Modern Self: Cultural Amnesia, Expressive Individualism, and the Road to Sexual Revolution* (Wheaton, IL: Crossway, 2020); Rod Dreher, *The Benedict Option: A Strategy for Christians in a Post-Christian Nation* (New York, NY: Sentinel, 2017), esp. chap. 9, "Eros and the New Christian Counterculture". For a lively manifesto capturing this rising current of thought, see also Jonathon Van Maren, "How to Be a Counter-Revolutionary", *European Conservative*, January 17, 2022, https://europeanconservative.com/articles/commentary/how-to-be-a-counter-revolutionary/.

[11] In the U.K., Louise Perry, *The Case Against the Sexual Revolution* (Cambridge: Polity, 2022). For France, see Chantal Delsol, *La Fin de la Chrétienté* (Paris, France: CERF, 2021). In Germany, see Gabriele Kuby, *The Global Sexual Revolution: Destruction of Freedom in the Name of Freedom* (Brooklyn, NY: LifeSite/Angelico Press, 2015).

[12] Houellebecq may yet prove to be to this latest Industrial Revolution what Charles Dickens was to the first—the novelist who made it possible for people in polite society to grasp that the deleterious empirical record demanded social reform.

Also noteworthy is the attention being given to life *after* liberationism.[13] The mere appearance of this contrarian proposition marks another signal transition.[14] Ten years ago, for example, pornography was the object of near-total indifference, enforced by a libertarian-libertine coalition that effectively dismissed any criticism as retrograde. Today, smut's detractors include not only religious conscientious objectors, but celebrities and other witnesses deploring addiction, as well as a thriving self-help industry that affirms the substance's harm.[15]

In addition to new ideas and new activism, one more development casts doubt on the insistence that doctrine concerning the revolution is "settled". The #MeToo movement, analyzed in a couple of this book's chapters, raised the tantalizing possibility that not only traditionalists, but also nontraditionalists and antitraditionalists, might unite in understanding that men and women have entered systemic, unforeseen crisis. The macabre political theater of pro-abortion forces amounts to tacit proof for exactly such a conclusion. So does the amplified determination to shut down crisis pregnancy centers, and with them, the free diapers, clothing, medicine, sonograms, and other essential help to women and babies in need.[16] The more

[13] Scott Yenor, "Sexual Counter-Revolution", *First Things*, November 2021, https://www.firstthings.com/article/2021/11/sexual-counter-revolution.

[14] See, for example, Christine Emba, *Rethinking Sex: A Provocation* (New York, NY: Sentinel, 2022).

[15] See, for example, Sarah Ditum, "Porn Will Destroy You", *Unherd*, December 22, 2021, https://unherd.com/2021/12/porn-will-destroy-you/; and Herb Scribner, "6 Big-Time Celebrities Who Have Spoken Out Against Pornography", *Deseret News*, September 26, 2016, https://www.deseret.com/2016/9/27/20596808/6-big-time-celebrities-who-have-spoken-out-against-pornography.

[16] For a list of examples in the weeks following *Dobbs*, see Nicole Ault, "The Attacks on Crisis Pregnancy Centers", *Wall Street Journal*, June 20, 2022, https://www.wsj.com/articles/the-attacks-on-crisis-pregnancy-centers

such heartlessness abounds, the more others might come to question the outlook that leads to it.

These developments spell jeopardy for what once seemed to be an invincible consensus on the side of those who cheered the unfettered social order born nearly six decades ago. It does not look invincible anymore. To call the reckoning unfolding "inevitable" would be historicist hubris. Yet without doubt, society is closer to giving liberationism a second look than at any moment since the 1960s. For this reason, thinkers inside and outside of Catholic circles who long to soften up Christianity by deep-sixing certain teachings could not have chosen a worse time than now to press their case. Why support the revolution's infiltration of the Church, at exactly the moment a rising chorus of voices from all over are beginning to question its toxic fruits and to seek alternatives outside today's disorder?

A thorough reevaluation will take centuries. In the meantime, such analysts today and tomorrow should be consoled. Understanding what liberation has wrought remains vital humanitarian work. The social, political, and religious crises of this age are not itinerant blips on the road to unending progress. They are instead manifestations of a civilizational leap backward. As the epilogue summarizes:

> Our secularizing culture is not just any culture. No, our secularizing culture is an inferior culture. It is small of heart. It defines suffering down. It regards the victims of its social experiments not as victims, but as acceptable collateral damage justified by those experiments. This is

-janes-revenge-abortion-roe-v-wade-violence-destroyed-11655653644. See also Christopher Ault, "Elizabeth Warren Smears Pro-Life Charities", *Wall Street Journal*, July 5, 2022, https://www.wsj.com/articles/elizabeth -warren-smears-pro-life-charities-mothers-maternity-homes-children-baby -pregnancy-center-11657053639.

secularism's unspoken secret. It is also secularism's greatest vulnerability.

That conviction has spurred this book, and its predecessor, into being. May the evidence presented inform believers and unbelievers alike, and strengthen the resolve of those tending the wounded.

PART I

THE FALLOUT CONTINUES

I

More Paradoxes of the
Sexual Revolution

Begin with a broad and uncontroversial formulation. The "revolution" refers to the changes in sexual behavior and mores following the widespread adoption and approval of reliable artificial contraception in the early 1960s. The first accelerant is the birth control pill, approved by the FDA in 1963 and widely dispersed in the population thereafter. The second accelerant is the legalization of abortion on demand in 1973 via *Roe v. Wade*—a development that approval of the Pill made all but inevitable.

Modern contraception and legalized abortion changed not only behavior, but also attitudes. Around the world, social tolerance of nonmarital sex in various forms has risen alongside these other changes, for reasons both intuitively transparent and empirically verifiable.[1]

Apart from the internet, it is hard to name any other single phenomenon since the 1960s that has reshaped the human race around the planet more profoundly than this metamorphosis. In the decades to follow, global Communism, and with it Marxism-Leninism, would crumble under the Velvet Revolutions. Nations around the world would be roiled by wars, economic shocks, terrorism,

[1] See, for example, Mary Eberstadt, *Adam and Eve after the Pill* (San Francisco, CA: Ignatius Press, 2012), chap. 8, 134–58.

31

civil unrest and violence, and a global pandemic on a scale unknown in over a century. The internet would change forever the ways that people shop, read, socialize, date, and marry (or not) and raise children (or not). Even so, for sheer systemic change remaking personal and national topographies across Planet Earth, the sexual revolution endures as a force of modernity second to none.

Some of its seismic effects are well-known. Female fertility control and fertility postponement have leveled the playing fields in the paid marketplace between women and men for the first time in history. Women now outnumber men as both matriculants and graduates of higher education. The sundering of procreation and recreation has conferred on the daughters of Eve freedoms such as they have never known before.[2]

At the same time, another side of the ledger continues to be ignored by a society mesmerized by career success and a la carte pleasure. With every passing year, evidence accumulates that the effects of widespread contraception have trickled deep below the surface of life, destabilizing the ground on which modern men and women stand. Consider as evidence five ways in which the revolution has reconfigured preexisting reality—five seeming paradoxes that point to its power, and in particular, to its awe-inspiring destructive power.

One anecdote helps to capture the scale of that change in miniature. I grew up in a series of hamlets and villages

---

[2] For a boosterish account, see, for example, Gail Collins, *When Everything Changed: The Amazing Journey of American Women from 1960 to the Present* (New York, NY: Little, Brown and Company, 2009). For a critique, see Mary Eberstadt, "Hear Me Roar", *Claremont Review of Books* 10, no. 3 (Summer 2010). For a prescient, earlier argument against the claim that sexual liberation has enhanced female happiness, see Midge Decter, *The New Chastity and Other Arguments against Women's Liberation* (London: Wildwood House, 1973).

scattered across beautiful and forbidding upstate New York—north of the Hudson River Valley, a planet away from New York City, in the area previously known as the Leatherstocking Region, because author James Fenimore Cooper set his classic American stories of early frontier adventure there. This was, and still is, rural, blue-collar country. It was the kind of setting in which more local boys in the 1960s went to Vietnam than to college. In many ways, sociological details of this area remain the same as they were in the 1960s—with one massive exception, the family thing.

In the 1960s, most men in this area worked as manual laborers, mainly on farms or in local copper and silver mills. Many women, if married, worked at home rather than in the paid marketplace. Most nuclear families were still intact, religious and nonreligious alike.[3] Also salient, this was not a particularly observant area of the country. The majority of residents were mainline Protestants, less than 10 percent were Catholic, and the local churches did not overflow on Sunday or any other day.

One vivid memory from childhood amounts to what psychologists call a "flashbulb moment" about the transformation America was about to undergo. In 1972, a teenaged girl down the street became pregnant. The baby's father was a young soldier, newly returned from the war. The town gossips were up in arms—because it turned out that he didn't plan to marry the girl. In those days, that was considered shocking. Although pregnant brides were hardly unknown, including teenaged pregnant brides, men who did not marry pregnant girlfriends were regarded almost universally as objects of opprobrium. So local tongues wagged.

---

[3] Throughout elementary school, for example, only one student in my grade had a last name different from that of her parents.

Eventually, this girl delivered the baby somewhere else, whereupon adoption followed. She came back to the area and finished high school without visible stigma. But the disapproval that does endure in memory was the other one: social disapproval of her boyfriend. The idea that he should have taken responsibility, which the majority of adults in that era and place believed, was then palpable in the tiny town.

Yet today, that same conviction is as foreign as the notion of an unwed mother going away to have a baby. Both conventions, along with others about family—and what men, especially, owed to family—vanished long ago into the cyclone of the revolution.

Now fast-forward some twenty years. In the early 1990s, I went back to upstate New York for a visit and met with a former high school teacher. She estimated that among that year's two hundred or so seniors, around one-third of the girls were pregnant. Not one was married. And doubtless there were other pregnancies besides the visible ones. From one scandalous pregnancy in a rural public high school in the 1970s to many nonscandalous pregnancies in that same school by the 1990s: this is one snapshot showing how liberationism has reconfigured America. It also leads us to the first of several paradoxes about that same tectonic shift.

If the foundation of the revolution was the availability of cheap, reliable birth control, why the unprecedented rise in both abortions and pregnancies outside of marriage?

This is a profoundly consequential question. After all, when contraception became commonplace, many people of goodwill defended it precisely because they thought it would render abortion obsolete. Margaret Sanger is one prominent example. Though her views on abortion seem to have fluctuated, she argued consistently for contraception on the ground that it would put abortion out of business.[4] She was making what might once have seemed like a commonsense point: reliable contraception would prevent abortion. A great many people, both before and after the 1960s, have believed something similar.

But the empirical record since the 1960s overrules this common conjecture: rates of contraception, abortion, and out-of-wedlock births all skyrocketed simultaneously. In 1996, a group of economists including Nobel Prize winner George A. Akerlof spelled out the meaning of these concomitant explosions with admirable clarity:

> Before the sexual revolution, women had less freedom, but men were expected to assume responsibility for their welfare. Today women are more free to choose, but men have afforded themselves the comparable option. "If she is not willing to have an abortion or use contraception," the man can reason, "why should I sacrifice myself to get married?" By making the birth of the child the physical choice of the mother, the sexual revolution has made marriage and child support a social choice of the father.[5]

In other words, contraception led to more pregnancy and more abortion because it eroded the so-called shotgun wedding—the idea that men had equal responsibility for an unplanned pregnancy, per the anecdote mentioned earlier.

Another theory about why contraception failed to prevent abortion comes from Scott Lloyd, writing in the *National Catholic Bioethics Quarterly*. Using studies and

[4] "No one can doubt that there are times where an abortion is justifiable but they will become unnecessary when care is taken to prevent conception. This is the only cure for abortions." (Margaret Sanger, *Family Limitation*, 8th ed. rev. [1918]), The Margaret Sanger Papers Project, New York University, https://sanger.hosting.nyu.edu/articles/ms_abortion/.

[5] George A. Akerlof, Janet L. Yellen, and Michael L. Katz, "An Analysis of Out-of-Wedlock Childbearing in the United States", *Quarterly Journal of Economics* 111, no. 2 (May 1996): 277–317, https://doi.org/10.2307/2946680.

statistics from the abortion industry itself, he (like others) argues that contraception leads to abortion—not inevitably in individual cases, of course, but repeatedly and reliably as twinned social phenomena:

> The bottom line is this: contraceptives do not work as advertised, and their failure is at the heart of the demand for abortion. Contraception enables sexual encounters and relationships that would not have happened without it. In other words, when couples use contraception, they agree to sex when pregnancy would be a problem. This leads to a desire for abortion.[6]

To grasp these perhaps counterintuitive developments with hindsight is to understand what most people present at the creation of this new order could not have known—namely, just how misplaced their optimism would turn out to be. Operating in good faith, some hoped that mankind would master these new technologies and that they would prove to be social goods. But men and women alive today, by contrast, possess a wealth of empirical evidence showing that a different and darker storyline has taken shape.

The sexual revolution was supposed to liberate women. The second paradox is that it has become harder for them to have what most women say they want: marriage and a family. Even today, female desires for home and hearth remain mostly unchanged from yesteryear. Women from across the political spectrum continue to cite marriage as a cherished priority.[7] They also agree that marrying and

[6] Scott Lloyd, "Can We Be Pro-Life and Pro-Contraception?", *National Catholic Bioethics Quarterly* 15, no. 2 (Summer 2015).

[7] See "The vast majority of unmarried adults desire eventual marriage", Mark Regnerus et al., *Relationships in America* (Austin, TX: Austin Institute for the Study of Family and Culture, 2014), 39, archived at https://web.archive.org/web/20220305220607/https://relationshipsinamerica.com/pdf/Relationships%20in%20America%202014.pdf.

mating for life has become more difficult than it used to be.[8] This is one reason why commercial surrogacy and the freezing of human eggs have come to be unremarkable—in the case of the latter, with the enthusiastic endorsement of corporate America, which often bankrolls that procedure so as not to interrupt the bottom line. The stated purpose of these innovations—besides the profits that accrue from uninterrupted careerism—is to extend the horizon of natural fertility so that women enjoy more options and "have more time" to find husbands and family. Like contraception and abortion on demand, the commodification of eggs is said to empower women and increase their control.

Yet paradoxically, many women find themselves less able than ever to get married, stay married, and have a family. This preoccupation echoes across media and social media, in headlines like "Eight Reasons Why New York Women Can't Get a Husband" (*New York Post*, March 12, 2014) or "Why College-Educated Women Can't Find Love" (*Daily Beast*, September 7, 2015) and in other stories worrying over the receding prospects for marriage.

Social science has thrown light onto the reality behind these apprehensions too. In his book *Cheap Sex: The Transformation of Men, Marriage, and Monogamy*, sociologist Mark Regnerus deploys economics to explain the postrevolutionary sexual market, aided by a formidable supply of new data. The essence of his argument is this: "To plenty of women, it appears that men have a fear of commitment. But men, on average, are not afraid of commitment. The story is that men are in the driver's seat in the marriage market and are optimally positioned to navigate it in a way that

---

[8] See, for example, Erin Coulehan, "Here's Why Millennials Are Getting Married Later Than Ever", *Cosmopolitan*, February 16, 2016, https://www.cosmopolitan.com/sex-love/news/a53741/heres-why-were-getting-married-later-than-ever/.

privileges their (sexual) interests and preferences."[9] In other words, the same force that rendered the shotgun wedding obsolete has gone on to empower men, not women.

One of the economists cited by Mark Regnerus, Timothy Reichert, wrote, using the tools of econometrics, a similar analysis of the revolution called "Bitter Pill", in the journal *First Things*.[10] Mining data from the 1960s onward, Reichert deduced that "the contraceptive revolution has resulted in a massive redistribution of wealth and power from women and children to men." He specified: "More technically, artificial contraception sets up what economists call a 'prisoner's-dilemma' game, in which each woman is induced to make decisions rationally that ultimately make her, and all women, worse off."

And in that cultural mainstream, the fact that many men do not settle down, marry, and start families is a constant, fretful preoccupation. It is why the phrase "Peter Pan syndrome" was coined in the 1980s; why "failure to launch" became common shorthand in the 2000s and beyond; and why "manolescent", "soy boy", and related denigrations have lately become nouns in the *Urban Dictionary*.

These additions to the vernacular have the same origin: diminished incentives for men to marry, due to the flooded sexual marketplace of potential partners—"cheap sex", as Regnerus' title has it. This outcome, too, is not one that people who cheered on the revolution in the 1960s foresaw. There are more.

A third paradox has become the dominant social media soap opera of our time, one that goes like this: The revolution was supposed to empower women. Instead, in

---

[9] Mark Regnerus, *Cheap Sex: The Transformation of Men, Marriage, and Monogamy* (New York, NY: Oxford University Press, 2017), 39.

[10] Timothy Reichert, "Bitter Pill", *First Things*, May 2010, https://www.firstthings.com/article/2010/05/bitter-pill.

addition to making marriage harder for many women to achieve, it also licensed sexual predation on a scale not seen outside of conquering armies.

Take Hugh Hefner, founder of *Playboy*, who died in 2017. His commercial empire was founded on pornographic photos of a great many women. He made himself an exemplar of his own vaunted ethos—the "Playboy philosophy" of life as a modern bon vivant including, of course, easy sex and plenty of it. The new libertine glamor caught on quickly. Back then, and for many years thereafter, few could have known the sordid truths about the exploitation behind the slick advertising; these would only emerge later thanks to first-person accounts from the Playboy "mansion".[11]

Nonetheless, when Hefner went on to his reward, feminists showered praise on this apostle of the revolution. Why? Because he cloaked his predatory designs in the language of progressivism. As a writer for *Fortune* summarized the record, "*Playboy* published its first article supporting the legalization of abortion in 1965, eight years before the *Roe v. Wade* decision that permitted the practice—and even before the feminist movement had latched onto the cause. It also published the numbers of hotlines that women could call and get safe abortions."[12]

---

[11] See, for example, Holly Madison, *Down the Rabbit Hole: Curious Adventures and Cautionary Tales of a Former Playboy Bunny* (New York, NY: Dey Street Books, 2015); and Izabella St. James, *Bunny Tales: Behind Closed Doors at the Playboy Mansion* (Philadelphia, PA: Running Press Adult, 2006); see also Carla Howe, "Another Playboy Bunny Exposes Grim Life with Hugh Hefner", *GQ Australia*, March 1, 2016. In 2022, A&E released and then expanded its documentary series *Secrets of Playboy*, which became A&E's most-watched series in over five years. Elizabeth Wagmeister, "'Secrets of Playboy' Hugh Hefner Series Gets More Episodes", *Variety*, March 7, 2022, https://variety.com/2022/tv/news/secrets-of-playboy-hugh-hefner-1235197604/.

[12] Claire Zillman, "How Hugh Hefner Used a Sexist Magazine to Champion Women's Reproductive Rights", *Fortune*, September 28, 2017, https://fortune.com/2017/09/28/hugh-hefner-death-playboy-womens-rights/.

In sum, Hefner's support for these causes appears inextricably tied up with his desire to live in a way that exploited women. This same Siamese twinning joins many of the secular sex scandals that exploded across the news from 2017 onward concerning predatory men, allegedly predatory men, and women who claimed to have been duped by them—also known as the #MeToo movement. One does not need to hazard the innocence or guilt of any given man who figured into the scandals to spy the bigger picture here: these stories revealed the same strategic role occupied by abortion for men who objectify women and disdain monogamy. Without the backup plan of fetal liquidation, where would such men be? In court, and paying child support.

More and more thinkers are coming to the same conclusion. The new utopianism did not deliver on its promises to women; instead, it further enabled men—especially men with lousy intentions. As Francis Fukuyama, a nonreligious social scientist, observed presciently in his 1999 book *The Great Disruption*:

> One of the greatest frauds perpetrated during the Great Disruption was the notion that the sexual revolution was gender-neutral, benefiting women and men equally.... In fact the sexual revolution served the interests of men, and in the end put sharp limits on the gains that women might otherwise have expected from their liberation from traditional roles.[13]

Thus, some nonreligious thinkers are beginning to grasp more clearly what some religious leaders have been saying

---

[13] Francis Fukuyama, *The Great Disruption: Human Nature and the Reconstitution of Social Order* (New York, NY: Free Press, 1999), 121–22.

all along. The revolution effectively democratized sexual predation. No longer did one have to be a king, or a master of the universe, to abuse or harass women in unrelenting, serial fashion. One only needed a world in which women would be assumed to use contraception, with abortion as a backup plan. That many would simultaneously be deprived by the shrinking family of male relatives would turn out to be advantageous as well. Jeffrey Epstein's outsized procurement, to name one obvious example, was reported to rely on the active pursuit of fatherless girls.[14] The social disorder delivered after the 1960s has been the gift that keeps on giving for exploitative men.

A fourth paradox is overdue for inspection: the effect of the revolution on Christianity itself, about which more will be said ahead. The struggle over what to do about the revolution has had two main effects: it has simultaneously polarized the churches from within, even as it has created tighter ties among different denominations than existed before.

In 2004, for example, a book by Stephen Bates about strife within the Anglican Communion, *A Church at War*, summarized the argument on its back cover: "Will the politics of sex tear Anglicans and Episcopalians apart?"[15] A few years later, writing on the same subject in *Mortal Follies: Episcopalians and the Crisis of Mainline Christianity*, William Murchison concluded with this observation: "For Episcopalians, as for large numbers of other Christians, the paramount issues are sex and sexual expression,

[14] Kate Briquelet and Jamie Ross, "Ghislaine Maxwell, Jeffrey Epstein's Confidante, Caught by the FBI in New Hampshire", *Daily Beast*, July 2, 2020, https://www.thedailybeast.com/ghislaine-maxwell-jeffrey-epsteins-confidante-arrested-by-the-fbi-report-says.

[15] Stephen Bates, *A Church at War: Anglicans and Homosexuality* (London: I.B. Tauris, 2004).

neither viewed by the culture as means to a larger end but as *the* end."[16] In his 2015 book *Onward: Engaging the Culture without Losing the Gospel*, Southern Baptist leader Russell D. Moore reflected similarly on the tension between evangelical progressives and traditionalists, concluding that "when it comes to religion in America at the moment, progress always boils down to sex."[17]

This, too, is a record seen best in hindsight. Like other optimists present at the revolution's creation, many Christians hoped to render it a force for good. Instead, accommodation yielded divisiveness at best, and the wholesale collapse of doctrine at worst. Those calling on Christianity to "loosen up" were in retrospect firing the opening shots in today's figurative civil war within the faith and across the denominations, as chapters 8 through 10 document in detail.

As each chapter in this book goes to show, the sexual revolution did not stop at sex. Presumptively private transactions between individuals have paradoxically gone on to reconfigure not only family life, but the wider economic, social, and political spheres inhabited by the revolution's heirs.

Some of these effects are economic. Smaller and more fractured families have put unprecedented pressure on the welfare states of the West by reducing the tax base required to sustain them. Smaller families have also meant that the state becomes a cradle-to-grave substitute, picking up slack left by diminishing numbers of caregivers. Since married men consistently work and earn more than their unmarried counterparts, the continuing decline of marriage implies

[16] William Murchison, *Mortal Follies: Episcopalians and the Crisis of Mainline Christianity* (New York, NY: Encounter Books, 2009), 203.

[17] Russell D. Moore, *Onward: Engaging the Culture without Losing the Gospel* (Nashville, TN: B&H Publishing Group, 2015).

lower economic productivity. Meanwhile, both private and public social services are chronically strained by increases in truancy, crime, substance abuse, and mental illness among young people, which are all linked to the rising number of fatherless homes.

Other outcomes, about which we will also hear more in chapters ahead, are social, such as the sharp rise in the numbers of people living alone or reporting greatly reduced human contact or other measures that make up the field of "loneliness studies", which was a burgeoning area of sociology across the countries of the West even before the pandemic made loneliness a curse common to all. Sharing the same root as burgeoning loneliness is another crisis proliferating across the same societies: a shortage of caregivers for the elderly. Though many fretful stories have been dedicated to that concern, especially during and after the COVID-19 pandemic, it is worth asking whether this crisis would exist on anything like today's scale if empty cradles had not become the norm.[18]

Then there is the spiritual fallout, the subject of several chapters to follow. As demonstrated in chapter 3, "From Revolution to Dogma: The Zealous Faith of Secularism", the revolution has also given rise to a new secularist, quasi-religious faith—the most potent such body of rival beliefs to Christianity since Marxism-Leninism. According to this new faith, there is no clear moral standard surrounding sex beyond the issue of consent (adult consent—again, for now). In this parallel universe to Christianity that has become the most commonly visited universe for many people, Christian and non-Christian alike, the sexual

---

[18] See, for example, Rhitu Chatterjee, "There's a Critical Shortage of Nursing Home Staff", *NPR*, February 6, 2022, Weekend Edition Sunday, https://www.npr.org/2022/02/06/1078634099/theres-a-critical-shortage-of-nursing-home-staff.

revolution amounts to a founding revelation—one that is off-limits for revision, no matter its consequences.

It has taken over sixty years for opinion to realign about just *some* of the revolution's negative legacy. It may take sixty more, or a hundred or two, for an unflinching accounting in full. As noted in the introduction, revisionist thinking about the revolution's effects in the world has only just begun.

And yet, opinion moves. In 1953, when the first issue of *Playboy* arrived on newsstands, many people wanted to believe its hype about enhancing the sophistication and urbanity of American men. By today, it is harder to pretend that the mainstreaming of pornography has been anything but a disaster for romance, and a prime factor in today's breakups and sexual consumerism. In 1973, even supporters of *Roe v. Wade* could not have imagined the evidence to come: some sixty-three million unborn human beings in the United States; and gendercide, or the selective killing of unborn girls for *being* girls, in various nations around the world, also numbering in the millions. Nor could supporters back then have imagined the technological leap that would unveil the truth about abortion once and for all: the sonogram.

These and other pertinent realities amount to mere drops on the revolution's bedrock. But with enough time, water does shape stone. To face facts squarely, and use them to tell a truthful story, is not to deliver a jeremiad. It is to empower. And the first step is ceasing to pretend that the empirical and historical records are other than what they are.

PART II

WHAT IS THE REVOLUTION DOING TO SOCIETY?

2

The New Intolerance

Postrevolutionary revisionism must take into account not only the fates of modern men and women, but also the profound reconfiguration of elementary facts of Western life during the decades since the 1960s. These transformations are the subjects of this chapter and the two that follow.

One such change, and a particularly momentous one, is something no one saw coming: the fact that liberationism would give rise to punitive new speech codes.

In November 2014, Cardinal Walter Kasper gave a talk at the Catholic University of America in which he said, "Mercy has become the theme of [Pope Francis'] pontificate.... With this theme, Pope Francis has addressed countless individuals, both within and without the Church.... He has moved them intensely, and pierced their hearts." The cardinal added, "Who among us does not depend on mercy? On the mercy of God, and of merciful fellow man?"[1] Such questions go straight to the core of the clash between liberationist ideology and religious freedom. Pope Francis and Cardinal Kasper and other spiritual leaders teach that mercy means meeting people where they

[1] Vinnie Rotondaro, "Cardinal Kasper: Pope Francis 'Does Not Represent a Liberal Position, but a Radical Position'", *National Catholic Reporter*, November 7, 2014, https://www.ncronline.org/news/people/cardinal-kasper-pope -francis-does-not-represent-liberal-position-radical-position.

live. Let us apply that counsel to the present and examine where many Christians in America and Europe and other places live today *because* they are Christians.

We are not speaking here of the believers around the globe risking mortal harm for the sake of their faith, but about something else: the slow-motion marginalizing and penalizing of the faithful on the very doorsteps of the churches of North America, Europe, and elsewhere, in societies that are the very historical strongholds of political and religious liberty.

Men and women of faith in these societies are well-off, compared to others. At the same time, their world is more socially iniquitous than it used to be. There is no mercy in putting butchers and bakers and candlestick makers in the legal dock for refusing to renounce their religious beliefs. There is no mercy in stalking and threatening Christian pastors for *being* Christian pastors, or in casting out social scientists who turn up unwanted facts, or in telling a flight attendant she can't wear a crucifix, or in persecuting organizations that do charitable work—but the new intolerance does these things. There is no mercy in yelling slurs at anyone who points out that the sexual revolution has been flooding the public square with problems for a long time now and that, in fact, some people out there are drowning—but slurs are fundamental to the new intolerance.

Above all, there is no mercy in slandering religious believers by saying that they "hate" certain people when in fact they do not or that they are "phobes" of some kind when in fact they are not. This, too, happens all over public space these days. This, too, is change for the worse.

The new intolerance has also been recognized by those speaking for the Church. As Bishop Mario Toso, secretary of the Pontifical Council for Justice and Peace, put it in a statement to the Organization for Security and Co-operation in Europe in 2013, long before "cancel culture" became a commonplace, "Intolerance in the name of 'tolerance' must be named for what it is and publicly condemned."[2] The phenomenon he identified can be distilled into five essential facts.

The first is that the new intolerance is not just a Christian problem. It is an everybody problem. One should not have to say—though the new intolerance forces one to say—that simple decency demands noncooperation with the maligning of others. As it happens, Christianity provides a robust moral vernacular for the rightness of resisting injustice. Even so, standing against slurs and innuendo is no mere religious quirk.

The new intolerance is also an everybody problem in another sense. Like related cultural unleashings, it will not stop at today's courthouse door. It will want more victims. Nobody's free speech is safe when mini-Robespierres write the rules. That includes people who now *think* they are safe because they have preemptively accommodated prevailing dogma and silenced themselves. Practicing Christians who refuse to recant are on the front lines of the new intolerance today. But where they stand now, others will soon. Some already do.

Tomorrow's scapegoat might be someone with no religious beliefs whatsoever, who draws the line at, say, the legalization of polygamy. Or at lowering the age of consent, as has happened in a number of countries farther along than our own in acquiescing to the sexual revolution's demands. Or at allowing biological men into areas once reserved for biological women, as has happened with

[2] Adelaide Mena, "Holy See Decries Intolerance 'in the Name of Tolerance'", *Catholic News Agency*, May 29, 2013, https://www.catholicnewsagency.com/news/27327/holy-see-decries-intolerance-in-the-name-of-tolerance.

the uproar over so-called TERFs.[3] Other people might think to object to related experiments, once more on nonreligious grounds—such as the womb trafficking of poor Third World women to manufacture babies for rich Westerners. Or to offer another example easily imagined: feminists who are otherwise on amiable terms with libertarianism might come to see, as has happened across the years, that pornography harms the interests of women and men alike, and ought to be less ubiquitous—especially the violent, sadistic, misogynistic pornography characteristic of the internet. If and when any such people do such things, the new intolerance seeks to ostracize them, just as it has other dissenters from the sexual revolution's *desiderata*. As more citizens fall victim, a growing secular chorus has come to denounce cancel culture.[4] This is all to the good.

At the same time, the new intolerance remains an everybody problem for one more reason that secular critics have not acknowledged, and should: it penalizes people who are a clear net-plus for society—people who spend their days helping the poor, clothing the naked, feeding the hungry, caring for the cast-off, and otherwise trying to live out the Judeo-Christian code of mercy. More and more, these Good Samaritans are witnesses to a wicked truth: the new intolerance makes it harder to help the poor and needy. And concern for the poor is not just some boutique Christian fillip—at least, it is not supposed to be.

---

[3] "Transgender-Exclusionary Radical Feminist". See, for example, Julie Compton, "'Pro-Lesbian' or 'Trans-Exclusionary'? Old Animosities Boil into Public View", *NBC News*, January 14, 2019, https://www.nbcnews.com/feature/nbc-out/pro-lesbian-or-trans-exclusionary-old-animosities-boil-public-view-n958456.

[4] See, for example, *Harper's*, "A Letter on Justice and Open Debate", signed by leading liberals in the United States and elsewhere, July 7, 2020, https://harpers.org/a-letter-on-justice-and-open-debate/.

Fact two about the new intolerance: it is different from what has come before. Reflecting several years ago in the *Wall Street Journal* on the galloping revival of anti-Semitism in parts of Western Europe, Rabbi Jonathan Sacks drew some interesting distinctions.[5] At one time, he pointed out, the Jews of Europe were hated for their religion. In the nineteenth and twentieth centuries, they were hated for their so-called race, and not only under National Socialism. In our own day, he continued, the main reason for anti-Semitism is something else again: hatred of the fact of their nation-state, Israel. Thus, one enduring hatred, anti-Semitism, consists of different variations on the theme.

In an analogous way, what might be called the varieties of anti-Christianity can also be distinguished over the centuries. One current form is the antipathy across Western Europe to acknowledging the Continent's religious roots. Scholar Joseph Weiler has gone so far as to call this Christophobia.[6] Other instantiations have abounded. The Romans persecuted Christianity because of the threat it posed to society and state. Friedrich Nietzsche and like-minded philosophers charged it with holding back human progress. Nazis and Communists killed and persecuted believers because they correctly saw in Christianity a mortal competitor to totalitarianism. (In time, a country called Poland and a saint called John Paul II would vindicate their apprehension.) And Christians themselves have found ample opportunities over the centuries to hate each other, usually over points of doctrine, many of which can now seem remote.

---

[5] Jonathan Sacks, "Europe's Alarming New Anti-Semitism", *Wall Street Journal*, October 2, 2014, https://www.wsj.com/articles/europes-alarming-new-anti-semitism-1412270003?page=1

[6] Matthew Schmitz, "Does It Make Sense to Speak of 'Christophobia'?", *First Things*, November 29, 2012, https://www.firstthings.com/blogs/firstthoughts/2012/11/does-it-make-sense-to-speak-of-christophobia/.

The new intolerance facing Western religious believers today differs from these variations. It is not an intellectual or a philosophical force. As the immortal character Jeeves once remarked of Bertie Wooster in a P. G. Wodehouse story, the new intolerance is in fact mentally negligible. It is hardly about ideas at all. It is instead something very specific, taken from playbooks that nobody should be proud of studying. It is about using intimidation, humiliation, censorship, and self-censorship to punish those who think differently.

Enter another witness. An American writer involved in several charities lately confided that his biggest fear is that his children will someday grow to hate him because they will be ostracized on account of their religion. If a Christian as committed as *he* is can't help thinking that way, what does that tell us about many millions of other parents? What will they decide about the religious upbringing of their children, in an age when taking them to church might get them laughed at, and maybe much worse? Anyone concerned about secularization has to be concerned about the new intolerance—because the new intolerance will *cause* secularization, by making people fear for themselves and for those they love. As argued elsewhere, this dynamic is manifestly operative on American and other campuses, where it amounts to one more unseen force driving churched students away from church.[7]

The new intolerance gives intimidated souls backhanded cultural permission to abandon religious practice. It is no surprise that religiously unaffiliated "nones" abound from New York to Paris to Sydney to Buenos Aires and everywhere in between. The connection between rising social

[7] Mary Eberstadt, "From Campus Bullies to Empty Churches", *Intercollegiate Review*, July 24, 2015, https://isi.org/intercollegiate-review/from-campus-bullies-to-empty-churches/.

stigma and declining attendance at church has barely been plumbed. But it is plainly prodigious.

The fact that Christians who have *not* been scared away from church wish that all these facts were otherwise is poignant. It is also, of course, a strategic liability for the believers. Everyone wants to be loved—or at least not promiscuously hated. The new intolerance is able to exploit this ubiquitous desire and to use it to tear Christianity from within, as well as to isolate and frighten people in its way. This dual threat is what makes the new intolerance so lethal. Sociologist Robert Nisbet once remarked that boredom is the most underestimated force in human affairs. Perhaps so. But the desire not to be hated must run a close second.

This brings us to fact three about the new intolerance: it is dangerous not only for the obvious reason that it imposes censorship, but even more because it imposes self-censorship—even within the churches. Inside Christianity itself, the scramble over the "right side of history" turns a community of sinners united by the shared search for redemption into something very different: a discrete series of aggrieved factions, each clamoring for spiritual entitlement. It is institutionally ruinous.

Nor is surrender an option. The churches that have tried to protect themselves from intolerance by ceding to its demands are dying. They do not replace themselves literally or figuratively; their morale is low; some will not even exist a hundred years from now. Responding to intolerance with capitulation is like trying to put out a house fire by throwing dynamite at it.

Fact four about the new intolerance: it claims to command the moral high ground. In fact, it does not and cannot. In the name of the revolution defended by the new intolerance, unborn innocents are killed by the millions every year, overwhelmingly on the sole ground that they are inconvenient. The revolution singles out as particularly unwanted the fetuses who are female, millions more of whom are killed than males, to the apparent and bizarre indifference of activists who claim to advance female interests.

As already demonstrated, that same social order demanded by cancel culture et al. is no friend of the poor—far from it. Consider evidence from sociologist W. Bradford Wilcox and Robert I. Lerman's seminal work, *For Richer, for Poorer: How Family Structures Economic Success in America*. Among the arresting findings:

> We estimate that the growth in median income of families with children would be 44 percent higher if the United States enjoyed 1980 levels of married parenthood today. Further, at least 32 percent of the growth in family-income inequality since 1979 among families with children and 37 percent of the decline in men's employment rates during that time can be linked to the decreasing number of Americans who form and maintain stable, married families.[8]

The sexual revolution, in other words, has been driving one of the most divisive political issues in Western society today: income inequality. It has been driving the middle class into the ground. And in its name, a new kind of racialism now operates out in the open: rich white people who tell poorer black people, especially in Africa, that their lives will be better if they make fewer of themselves (a phenomenon that humorist P. J. O'Rourke has memorably dubbed "just enough of me, way too much of you").

Out there in the flooded public square, two visions compete for hearts and minds. Which one stands on higher ground?

---

[8] W. Bradford Wilcox and Robert I. Lerman, *For Richer, for Poorer: How Family Structures Economic Success in America* (Washington, DC: American Enterprise Institute and the Institute for Family Studies, October 28, 2014).

Recall what happened in 2010 under the Affordable Care Act, when the federal government of the United States decided to meet the demands of the revolution by mandating that health insurance cover contraception. The particular battle between the government and the Little Sisters of the Poor came straight out of central casting—from Hell. It was as if the producers of a movie had sat around pitching ideas that went like this: "I know! Let's do something really preposterous. Let's make the federal government beat up on nuns." And someone else says, "I know! Not just any nuns, but nuns who work with the destitute and outcast." And a third one says, "I know! I've got it! How about we have the government try and knee-cap ... the *Little Sisters of the Poor*?"

Of course, had any such meeting actually happened, everyone would have walked away from the project—because anyone in Hollywood could see that there would be no purchase in attacking the Little Sisters of the Poor; who would stand for it? But as it turned out, plenty of people were fine with all that—people marching to the new intolerance. This is only moral high ground if one is standing in a ditch.

The new intolerance makes the tired claim of standing on the right side of history. Here is one more proof, a new one, of why it fails. Of all the witnesses who can be produced to shut down the new intolerance, the most compelling may be the most hitherto unseen. These are the former victims of the sexual revolution themselves—the walking wounded coming in and out of those proverbial field hospitals, the people who are believers not because they want to jettison the Christian moral code, but because they want to do something more radical: live by it.

The truth that has not been reckoned with by religion's cultured despisers today is this: Christianity is being built more and more by these very witnesses—by people who have come to embrace the difficult and longstanding Christian rulebook not because they know nothing of the revolution and its fallout, but because they know all too much.[9]

There are other witnesses who plead openly for the Church to keep being a sign of contradiction—witnesses who must be heard at an hour when the Church has put questions of the family front and center. These are the conscientious objectors to the new intolerance, those who come forward to avow that they *do* have free will—no matter how many other people insist otherwise—and who are vilified for committing secular heresy. There are organizations like the Catholic group Courage, for men and women with same-sex attractions who desire to live chaste Christian lives, despite the nonstop recrimination aimed their way.

More and more sentinels come into view. Two of them attended a groundbreaking conference on the social costs of pornography at the Witherspoon Institute in Princeton, New Jersey, in 2008.[10] Each man testified before scores of strangers about what addiction to smut had cost him personally—mainly, the loss of love. Such people are indispensable witnesses to the rubble of the sexual revolution, and exceptionally courageous ones.

[9] See, for example, Luma Simms, "My Plea: I'm a Divorced and Remarried Mother. Please, Don't Change Church Practice", *First Things*, November 3, 2014, https://www.firstthings.com/web-exclusives/2014/11/my-plea; see also Louise Mensch, "I'm a Divorced Catholic. And I'm Sure It Would Be a Mortal Sin for Me to Take Communion", *Spectator*, October 4, 2014, https://www.spectator.co.uk/article/i-m-a-divorced-catholic-and-i-m-sure-it-would-be-a-mortal-sin-for-me-to-take-communion; and "Hope for Women in Hell", an interview by Rachel Marie Stone with former prostitute Anny Donewald, who has gone on to found a ministry for other women exploited by the so-called adult entertainment industry, *Christianity Today*, October 27, 2014, https://www.christianitytoday.com/ct/2014/october/hope-for-women-in-hell.html.

[10] See Mary Eberstadt and Anne Layden, *The Social Costs of Pornography: A Statement of Findings and Recommendations* (Princeton, NJ: Witherspoon Institute, 2010); James R. Stoner Jr. and Donna M. Hughes, eds., *The Social Costs of Pornography: A Collection of Papers* (Princeton, NJ: Witherspoon Institute, 2010).

All these men and women are living, human signs of contradiction to the times, and most especially to the new intolerance. They are part of the growing coalition of people who defend faith in all its thorniness *not* because they have known nothing else, but precisely because they *do* know the revolution. And they reject the idea of marching in lockstep with it.

One final reason beyond even the new intolerance suggests why those witnesses must all be heard, and not wrongly written off as losers to history. On June 10, 1194, a great fire swept through a prominent Romanesque cathedral in a town southwest of Paris. Its loss threatened to devastate people and towns for many miles around, and for many generations too. There must have been plenty of villagers living then who wanted to give up, declare disaster the existential winner, and go elsewhere.

What happened instead was, and remains, extraordinary by any standard. Those people and their leaders persevered and determined not to have their lives disfigured once and for all by disaster. In a remarkably short time, something mightier and even more magnificent was raised up in its place. That building is known as Notre-Dame de Chartres Cathedral. Among the most sublime creations on earth, it is the legacy of men and women in a particular time and place who had witnessed the signature disaster of their era—and who refused to resign themselves to it.

So too will the Church of tomorrow come to be built, not by partisans of the new intolerance, or by people who buckle to censorship or self-censorship; it will instead be laid stone by stone by some of the very people burned in the original fire. As real as the new intolerance is the emergent renewal movement that will end up its greatest contender.

3

From Revolution to Dogma:
The Zealous Faith of Secularism

To be Christian today is to be a sailor in search of an astro-labe, as profuse analyses go to show.[1] Small wonder—believers are in open, roiling, uncharted waters, so looking up to fixed points would help. One other way to orient ourselves is to peer down beneath the currents and to focus on the subterranean realignments beneath today's de-Christianizing Western landscape.

That deeper dive reveals that the United States and other nations rooted in Judeo-Christianity have entered a time of paganization—what might also be called "repaganization".

---

[1] In 2009, Richard John Neuhaus called this new place *American Babylon: Notes of a Christian Exile* (New York, NY: Basic Books, 2010). Rod Dreher speaks of *The Benedict Option: A Strategy for Christians in a Post-Christian Nation* (New York, NY: Sentinel, 2017). George Weigel calls for a new Great Awakening, and for another option named after Fr. Arne Panula, a tireless evangelizer who presided during his last ten years over the Catholic Information Center in Washington, D.C.; George Weigel, "Easter and the 'Panula Option'", *National Review*, April 15, 2017, https://www.nationalreview.com/2017/04/easter-joy-father-arne-panula-witness-christ/. Using T. S. Eliot as a touchstone, *First Things* editor R. R. Reno argues along a different track for *Resurrecting the Idea of a Christian Society* (Washington, DC: Salem Books, 2016). In *Strangers in a Strange Land*, Archbishop Charles J. Chaput develops an analogy between our time and that of the Book of Exodus (New York, NY: St. Martin's Press, 2019). In one more essential book, Anthony Esolen evokes the image of the phoenix with *Out of the Ashes: Rebuilding American Culture* (Washington, DC: Regnery Publishing, 2016).

The gravitational pull of traditional religion seems to be diminishing, even as a-religious and antireligious elements accumulate critical mass.

This repaganization is especially ascendant among the young. Its wider manifestations are now commonplace and include the proliferation of religious liberty court cases, legal and other attacks on Christian student groups at secular universities, demonization and caricature of religious believers across popular culture, intimidation aimed at those who defend Judeo-Christian morality, and other instances of what Pope Francis himself has dubbed the "polite persecution" of believers in advanced societies. Repaganization is also evident in the malignant conflation of Christianity with "hate speech", an ideological branding destined to unleash new forms of grief on believers in the time ahead.

So far, so familiar. According to one dominant paradigm shared by most people, the world is now divided into two camps: people of faith and people of no faith. But this either-or template is mistaken. Today's repaganization is driven above all by a new historical phenomenon: the development of a rival faith—a rival, *secularist* faith that sees Christianity as a competitor to be vanquished, rather than as an alternative set of beliefs to be tolerated in an open society.

It is true that several other, fellow-traveling gnostic enthusiasms have also taken on religious shape. Climate change, critical race theory, identity politics of the left and right: all continue to develop ritual and dogma; all point to their own horsemen of the Apocalypse; all qualify as what Joseph Bottum has dubbed "bastard Christianities".[2] Even

[2] Joseph Bottum, *An Anxious Age: The Post-Protestant Ethic and the Spirit of America* (New York, NY: Image Books, 2014).

so, one particularly ascendant sect now over half a century in the making dwarfs the rest. That is the increasingly systematic, zealous, secularist faith rooted in the sexual revolution itself. One cannot understand either the perils or opportunities of Christianity today without first understanding this developing, rival body of beliefs with which it contends.

Consider the scene on the steps of the Supreme Court of the United States on June 27, 2016, following the announcement of the decision in *Whole Woman's Health v. Hellerstedt*, a decision about Texas abortion clinics that amounted to a victory for proponents of abortion. The moment that decision was announced, exuberant irrationalism ruled. Videos documented the outdoor revelry that resulted, spilling from the court steps out into the nation's capital: a gyrating, weeping, waving, screaming sea of people, mostly women, behaving as if they were in the throes of religious ecstasy. They were intoxicated like maenads in the *Bacchae*.

Occam's Razor dictates that those activists *were* in religious ecstasy—*their* kind of religious ecstasy, in which abortion on demand becomes the gnostic equivalent of a central sacrament, the repetition of which is judged essential to their quasi-religious community.

Or consider another snapshot: the so-called Women's March on Washington on January 21, 2017, the day after the Inauguration of President Donald Trump. This public demonstration, too, was driven by secularist animus against perceived threats to the postrevolutionary social order, particularly access to abortion. Thus, the totemic hats used to brand the event were named not for any conventional political concern—jobs, taxes, defense, the economy, health care, immigration. To clinch the point, the only women disinvited from this supposedly universal "women's march" were pro-life.[3] When forced to choose between women and abortion on demand, the women in charge chose abortion. That happened because, within this new church of secularism, pro-life women, and men, amount to heretics: despised transgressors of a religious community's core teaching and norms.

The passion on public display before and after the leaked opinion in the 2022 case of *Dobbs v. Jackson Women's Health Organization* was of a piece with the same frenzy. This time around, fealty to abortion was spiced with real and threatened violence, ranging from increased vandalism, the doxing of the home addresses of some justices, chilling references on social media to their children and their children's schools, and a threat on the life of Justice Brett Kavanaugh.[4] Once again, the greater meaning of the menacing political theater was clear. Abortion is not treated by its proponents like any other political issue. It exerts talismanic power and demands unequivocal loyalty.

If the so-called right to choose were truly an exercise of choice—if the rhetoric of the people who defend it matched the reality of what they actually believe—one would expect its defenders to honor choosing against it here or there. But this does not happen; no "pro-choice" group holds up as an example any woman who chooses not to abort.

That this does not happen unveils something noteworthy. For secularist believers, abortion is not in fact a mere

---

[3] Leandra Bernstein, "More Pro-Life Groups Removed as Official Partners of the Women's March", *ABC*, January 18, 2017, https://wjla.com/news /local/more-pro-life-groups-removed-as-partners-of-the-womens-march.

[4] Jonathan Turley, "From Court Packing to Leaking to Doxing: White House Yields to a National Rage Addiction", *The Hill*, May 7, 2022, https:// thehill.com/opinion/judiciary/3480452-from-court-packing-to-leaking-to -doxing-white-house-yields-to-a-national-rage-addiction/.

"choice", as their values-free, consumerist rhetoric frames it. No, abortion is sacrosanct. It is a communal rite—one through which many novices are initiated into this new faith. The popular, internet-driven rage for "telling one's own abortion story"—the phenomenon known as #shoutyourabortion—illustrates this point. Each individual story is a secularist pilgrim's progress into a new religious community united by this bloody rite of passage.

Secularist progressivism, to repeat, has erected a church. Christianity today, like Christianity past and Christianity to come, contends with many enemies. But the adversary now inflicting maximal damage on the Church is not dreamed of in Horatio's philosophy. It is instead the absolutist defense of the sexual revolution by its faithful, and the chilling effect of their words and deeds on Christians themselves.

After all, believers are not heckled from Hollywood to Capitol Hill for feeding the hungry, visiting the sick, or clothing the naked. Bakers are not landing in court because of icing their treats with verses from the Song of Songs. The expressions of animosity now aimed against Christianity by this new secularist faith share a common denominator. They are rooted in secularist dogma about the sexual revolution, according to which that revolution is a great leap forward for mankind from which no one is allowed to look back.

This substitute religion pantomimes Christianity itself in fascinating ways. It offers a hagiography of secular saints, all patrons of the sexual revolution: proselytizers for abortion and contraception such as Margaret Sanger and Gloria Steinem. Between 1966 and 2015, Planned Parenthood conferred annual awards on pro-abortion journalists, politicians, activists, and others. These awards were known affectionately as the "Maggies", for Margaret Sanger—Planned Parenthood's "highest honor", in the organization's words—and they were granted in recent years to luminaries such as Nancy Pelosi and Hillary Clinton.[5]

This brings us to another feature of the new secularist faith: its lack of transparency. For decades, scholarship has established Sanger's moral roots in eugenics, her faith in the inferiority of certain other people, her cynical use of African American ministers to evangelize the black population about birth control in the hope of bringing their numbers down, and related beliefs out of favor today. Yet in a moment when Confederate statues are targets in the name of scrubbing racism from the public square, Margaret Sanger has remained largely immune from moral revisionism. Why? Because she is the equivalent of a secularist saint of the revolution, off-limits from second thoughts.

Protection and communal silence are also conferred upon pseudo-scientist Alfred C. Kinsey, founder of the Institute for Sex Research at Indiana University. His fabled "reports" on human sexuality included allowing so-called research "subjects" to inflict what is now called child sexual abuse. According to biographer James H. Jones, Kinsey also filmed sex acts of employees and subordinates, walked in on students as they showered, had sex with people involved in his "research", wrote letters of erotica to assistants and others, and otherwise appears to have fallen short of today's vaunted standards concerning harassment and consent.[6] Even before #MeToo became global shorthand, Kinsey's legacy would have long since been questioned by

[5] Kate Scanlon, "Planned Parenthood Quietly Stops Distributing Margaret Sanger Award", *National Catholic Register*, August 19, 2020, https://www.ncregister.com/news/planned-parenthood-quietly-stops-distributing-margaret-sanger-award.

[6] James H. Jones, *Alfred C. Kinsey: A Public/Private Life* (New York, NY: W. W. Norton, 1997).

reasonable people—were he anything but Kinsey, that is, a founding father of the new secularist faith.

This rival faith sports foreign "missionaries", too, in the form of progressive charities and international bureaucracies—those who carry word of the revolution, and the pseudo-sacraments of contraception and abortion, to women around the planet. The Bill and Melinda Gates Foundation, to name one prominent example, has made the provision of contraception a centerpiece of its overseas work. In 2015, it pledged $120 million in the hopes of limiting the fertility of "an additional 120 million women and girls in the poorest countries by 2020".[7]

Who, exactly, are these women? Judging by the photos on the Gates Foundation website, they do not hail from Iceland or Denmark. As the foundation explains, "Less than 20 percent of women in Sub-Saharan Africa and barely one-third of women in South Asia use modern contraceptives"—making these darker-skinned women targets of quasi-religious zeal.

In fact, preoccupation with the fertility of *certain other people* is a constant theme in the church of the new secularism. In July 2017, French president Emmanuel Macron revealed his own fealty to the faith when he dilated at an appearance in Germany, of all places, upon the "civilizational" challenges facing Africa, singling out for disapproval the fact that women in some countries still have "seven or eight children".[8] Elsewhere that same summer, Canada's minister of international development, Marie-Claude

[7] Bill & Melinda Gates Foundation, "No Time to Lose: Fulfilling Our Family Planning Promise to 120 Million Women", press release, November 12, 2015, https://www.gatesfoundation.org/Ideas/Media-Center/Press-Releases/2015/11/Family-Planning-Promise.

[8] Marisa Iati, "'Perfectly Educated' Women Don't Have Big Families, Macron Said. Then the Moms Spoke Up", *Washington Post*, October 19, 2018, https://www.washingtonpost.com/religion/2018/10/19/perfectly-educated-women-dont-have-big-families-macron-said-then-moms-spoke-up/.

Bibeau, called abortion "a tool to end poverty".[9] In 2009, Supreme Court Justice Ruth Bader Ginsburg made a similar slip in an interview with the *New York Times Magazine*, reflecting that "at the time Roe was decided, there was concern about population growth and particularly growth in populations that we don't want to have too many of."[10]

Again, it is the lack of transparency that makes this faith go round. Under any other circumstances, if well-heeled white people were to proclaim that the solution to the world's problems is to have fewer dark people, opprobrium would result. Yet in secular quarters, treasure and acclaim are showered on programs whose end result is exactly that: the diminishment of mostly black and brown families by mostly white population activists.

This is what happens when the cornerstone of one's religion is protection of the sexual revolution at all costs and the consequences—eugenics, violations, and other transgressions—be damned.

To understand just what today's Western Christians face, it helps to bring the hidden premises of this rival faith into the open. For example, when people say that they hope the Church changes its position on marriage or birth control, they are not talking about *one* religious faith— i.e., the Christian one. What they really mean is that they hope the Church will suborn or replace its own theology with the theology of the new church of secularism. Or when public figures say they are "privately opposed to abortion"—even as they vote for policies that will ensure its ubiquity—they are using language to conceal rather

[9] "Aid Minister Maintains Need for Abortion Rights Amid Bishops' Criticism", *CTV News*, July 11, 2017, https://www.ctvnews.ca/politics/aid-minister-maintains-need-for-abortion-rights-amid-bishops-criticism-1.3498137.

[10] Emily Bazelon, "The Place of Women on the Court", interview with Justice Ruth Bader Ginsburg, *New York Times Magazine*, July 7, 2009, https://www.nytimes.com/2009/07/12/magazine/12ginsburg-t.html.

than clarify their intention. What they really want is to enjoy a kind of dual religious citizenship, according to which they are "Catholic" or "Christian" under certain conditions and followers of the church of secularism in any circumstances bearing on the sexual revolution.

Of course this effort to keep a foot in both churches fails, as would any claim to being simultaneously Muslim and Buddhist, say. The attempt to enjoy dual religious citizenship, particularly among politicians and others in the public eye, should be understood for what it is: a stealth move to serve the secularist religious master at the expense of the competing, Christian one.

The fact that two faiths now vie for supremacy within the West also explains the vehemence aimed at public figures who are practicing Christians—in particular, practicing Catholics. In 2017, during the confirmation hearing of Judge Amy Coney Barrett for the Court of Appeals, several senators remarked upon and denounced her Catholic faith. The most telling rhetorical moment may have been Senator Dianne Feinstein's declaration that "the dogma lives loudly within you"—an expostulation more fitted to an exorcist preparing for battle with Satan than to an American elected official charged with ascertaining the judicial fitness of a candidate.[11] Thus, Senator Feinstein's otherwise bizarre interjection captured the truth in seconds: the so-called culture war is a contest of *contending* faiths.

What does this tour of the new church of secularism mean for those outside its congregation? First, Christians must grasp that something new has entered the American

[11] " 'The Dogma Lives Loudly in You', Democratic Senator on Amy Coney Barrett", *Guardian*, September 26, 2020, YouTube, https://www.youtube.com/watch?v=9mDQM1TzlAM.

religious scene. After great troubles, the United States has come to pride itself in the peaceful coexistence of multiple faiths and denominations. The rival church of secularism seeks no such comity, as today's unprecedented attacks on Christian schools, charities, colleges, homeschooling, and other works go to show. The new church of secularism serves a very jealous god. "Ecumenical" is not in its vocabulary.

Missionary exuberance also explains why the new secular faith has insinuated itself successfully into Christian institutions, and why this insinuation has been invariably destructive. At the micro level of personal behavior, the new faith tempts people toward disobedience and cafeteria Christianity. At the macro level, it is institutionally divisive. It turns the followers of Christ into political interest groups. The scramble over doctrine in the Catholic Church, conducted entirely by advocates who mistakenly believe that the dogmas of both faiths can be somehow reconciled, is a powerful example of the sexual revolution's virulent workings within Christianity itself.

Even so, the most insidious threat to the real Church, and even to religious liberty, is not the new secularist church in itself. The greater menace is self-censorship. There is understandable temptation among Christians to capitulate preemptively to this new faith, for all kinds of reasons: saving face, not being "judgy", preventing the ostracism of one's children. Even so, Christians need to know that the sex-fixated dogmas of this new faith require purposeful engagement, not accommodation.

This vocation of religious opposition is necessary not only for the protection of the Church, but also for the sake of the sexual revolution's real and many victims. The new church of secularism is rooted in a false anthropology that mismeasures human nature and deprives mankind of redemption, fomenting misery across generations. The malign consequences of secularist doctrine are playing out especially among the young. The scene on many American campuses, to offer one example, has become surreal, replete with demonstrations and high emotional drama and seemingly inexplicable animosities. But *why* are more and more students behaving so bizarrely in the first place?

Post-Pill, confusion rules the earth. Yet this ongoing catastrophe over the fundamental question of *who we are* also offers unique countercultural opportunities.

On closer inspection, for instance, the secularist church looks to be less than monolithic. Witness again how the conflagration that started with Hollywood mogul Harvey Weinstein has gone on to illuminate wrongdoing elsewhere, all of it premised on the notion that women are available for recreational sex anywhere and anytime. Meanwhile, new Catholic and other Christian associations proliferate on campuses, despite fierce secularist pushback.[12]

These and other platoons like them will transform the American landscape. They encourage the search for transcendence in a world where neo-paganism insists there is none. They push back against a critical vulnerability: the rival church of secularism shortchanges mankind. The human race, plodding and delinquent though it may be, perpetually shows signs of wanting more than the church of the new secularism can deliver.

---

[12] If the increase in "nones" is one emblematic story of our time, so too is the birth of countercultural campus communities like the Thomistic Institute, the Love and Fidelity Network, and Fellowship of Catholic University Students (FOCUS); the rise in high schools grounded in classical education; the Leonine Forum for young professionals in Washington, D.C., now expanded into New York, Chicago, and Los Angeles; related projects like the Tertio Millennio Seminar in Poland and the Free Society Seminar in Slovakia; and many other organic responses, both protective and proactive, to competition from the rival church of secularism.

Two such witnesses to that reality appeared in Washington, D.C., in 2017, in the middle of a heat wave. They had been in touch to discuss a documentary they were creating to coincide with the fiftieth anniversary of *Humanae Vitae*. Their studio in D.C. turned out to be their hotel room. The entourage for the shoot included their three very young children, with whom they took turns throughout the interview. They had made many sacrifices and traveled hundreds of miles because, they said, they were on a mission to tell the truth.

The young woman had grown up without knowing who her father was. Her mother, a radical feminist, raised her to fear and hate men. The young man came from Scandinavia and had grown up as secular as can be. Both, if encountered earlier in their lives, would have been categorized as "nones".

In their own estimations, these two people had escaped from behind enemy lines of the sexual revolution. Somehow, they found each other. Somehow, falling in love led them to question what had happened in their pasts. Somehow, they encountered a priest. Somehow, they read some countercultural books. And what with one improbable development and another, both ended up converting to Catholicism. They concluded that their vocations involved sharing with others the truths that they had discovered the hard way.

Archbishop Jose Gomez of Los Angeles has connected our moment in the West to Juan Diego's in Guadalupe, almost five hundred years ago.[13] Today's world, like Diego's, has raised up generations schooled in an inhuman account of human life. The resulting deformations are thick on the

---

[13] Archbishop Jose H. Gomez, "Such As We Are, Such Are the Times", speech to the Napa Institute, October 3, 2017, https://www.youtube.com/watch?v=otpXaK5c9co.

ground. Confusion cannot help but abound. Even so, the secularist faith is vulnerable for the same reasons that Marxism is: its promises are false, and its anthropology fallacious.

The church that the sexual revolution has built is thriving. But its pews are packed with casualties—every one of them, at least potentially, a convert waiting to happen, for the churches that do still believe in what the walking wounded need most: redemption.

4

Men Are at War with God

The contest between Christianity and its secular competitor is playing out across all the West's most valuable cultural real estate. It reveals itself in the social and civil penalties accumulating for violations of speech—the rough equivalent of falling asleep in church or swearing in public under Puritanism. It drives discussions in the United Nations, the European Union, and other bureaucracies that task themselves with writing these new religious norms into law. The same struggle joins thousands of skirmishes over ethnicity and identity playing out in America's classrooms, from college down to preschool.

Familiar though these flashpoints may be, they are also epiphenomena of an even more essential struggle. Aleksandr Solzhenitsyn famously defined the principal trait of the twentieth century in four words: "Men have forgotten God."[1] So far, the twenty-first century might be summarized in six: men are at war with God. Awakened from agnostic slumber by potent new ways of rationalizing temptation, mankind is at war with God over a question that reaches back to the beginning of time: Who, exactly, should have power over creation?

[1] Aleksandr Solzhenitsyn, "Acceptance Address" on receiving the Templeton Prize, May 10, 1983, https://www.templetonprize.org/laureate-sub /solzhenitsyn-acceptance-speech/.

Christianity and Judaism teach that the answer is God. The culture dominant in the West today teaches the opposite. It says that the creation of new life is ours to control—more precisely, that it is woman's to control. It says that we can dispose of life in the womb for any reason whatsoever, from simple whim to a preference for a boy rather than a girl. It goes further, saying that we can erase life on the basis of rationales that continue to expand. In Belgium, a middle-aged woman was euthanized because she was distraught over the surgeries done and chemicals taken in the vain hope that she could "change" her sex.[2]

How have postrevolutionary men and women reached the point where societies built on fealty to the Creator now repudiate creation itself?

The answer begins with a closer look at resistance to being designated a "creature" at all. Why? In part, because "creature" is a relational term—and many Western people now mature into a world without robust relational ties. Some do not know fathers, brothers, sisters, or extended family. Some do not even recognize themselves as male or female. The crushing loss of relationality at large makes any individual form of relationality harder to understand. After all, a world in which many people cannot even grasp their primordial ties to one another is one in which their failure to relate to something more abstract—God, say—is not exactly a surprise of the first order.

Consider the case via a syllogism. The sexual revolution led to the decline of the family. This weakening in turn has fueled the decline of organized religion. Both of these losses have left elephantine holes in the Western sense of

[2] "Belgian Helped to Die after Three Sex Change Operations", *BBC News*, October 2, 2013, https://www.bbc.com/news/world-europe-24373107.

self. As a result, many Western people now scramble to fill those vacancies with something else.

The revolution robbed many modern people of a familial identity. By spurring secularization, it also robbed them of a supernatural foundation. The first change cut their primordial horizontal ties; the second, their primordial vertical ones. As a result, many have been catapulted off to a place where gravity barely exists, and where the valence of others is too weak to exert effects.

The results of unnatural solitude are an established part of the scientific ledger—at least when it comes to other species. Longstanding experiments on nonhuman animals have demonstrated that artificial isolation from their own kind produces dysfunction.[3] What is not so well understood, and needs to be, is that mankind is running an analogous experiment on itself. The modern ecosphere is choked with indissoluble deposits that never before existed on the scale seen today.

Abortion, fatherlessness, divorce, single parenthood, childlessness, the imploding nuclear family, the shrinking extended family—all these phenomena have something in common. They are acts of human *subtraction*. Every one of them has the effect of reducing the number of people to whom we belong, and whom we can call our own. Psychologist Harry Harlow's deprivation experiments on rhesus monkeys are remembered today for the lifelong

---

[3] "The over 60-year NHP [nonhuman primate] studies shed lights on the understanding of the influences of EARE on physiological and behavioral development, including social behaviors (e.g., disturbance behavior, social deficiency, sexual behavior, etc.), learning and memory ability, brain structural and functional development (e.g., development of neurons and glia cells, neuroendocrine dysregulation, etc.)." Bo Zhang, "Consequences of Early Adverse Rearing Experience (EARE) on Development: Insights from Non-Human Primate Studies", *Zoological Research* 38, no. 1 (January 18, 2017):7.

consequences those creatures suffered when separated from their mothers, siblings, and the rest of monkey society.[4] When Western man looks in the mirror today, does he see their damaged ghosts standing beside him?

Outside the consciously religious communities of the counterculture, generational reality for almost everyone else in the West can be summarized in one word: *fewer*. Fewer brothers, sisters, cousins, children, grandchildren. Fewer people to play ball with, or talk to, or learn from. Fewer people to celebrate a birth; fewer people to visit one's deathbed. Splitting the human atom into recreation and procreation has produced a love deficit.

As individual lives become more disordered and bereft, so do our politics. The first use of the phrase "identity politics" appears in a manifesto published by radical African American feminists in 1977—just as the first generation born into the revolution was coming of age. The document in which it debuts, *The Combahee River Collective Statement*, is a poignant window onto modern times. It declares, in essence, that its signatories—all women—are giving up on the men in their lives. They are banding together for a future that does not include unreliable boyfriends and husbands.[5]

There is a straight line from that declaration of failure to the one uploaded by Black Lives Matter (BLM) in 2020 (and subsequently removed from its website), which likewise denied healthy relations between the sexes and within

[4] Harry F. Harlow, Robert O. Dodsworth, and Margaret K. Harlow, "Total Social Isolation in Monkeys" (lecture, *National Academy of Sciences*, Washington, DC, April 28, 1965), National Center for Biotechnology Information, https://www.ncbi.nlm.nih.gov/pmc/articles/PMC285801/pdf/pnas00159-0105.pdf.

[5] Combahee River Collective, *The Combahee River Collective Statement* (April 1977), Yale University, https://americanstudies.yale.edu/sites/default/files/files/Keyword%20Coalition_Readings.pdf.

the natural family and failed even to mention fathers or brothers. Both the Combahee River and BLM proclamations signify that political identity has become a substitute for familial and communal bonds. Both are rooted in a fury at creation itself—more specifically, an anger at the *disruption* of the natural order, which the creature now claims the right to reorder.

Facing these givens without blinkers, what lessons can be spied?

The first imperative is compassion. If Christianity, in particular, is to rebuild from the rubble, the faithful need to grasp what lies under those rocks: massive, often misunderstood or unseen suffering. This includes the suffering of people in factions that commonly oppose the Church. It has become easy to dismiss the public enactments of identity politics with derogatory terms like "snowflake", "coddled Millennial", and "spoiled brats". Easy—and wrong.

There is a common denominator beneath the bizarre rituals occurring on campuses and elsewhere, beneath an increasingly punitive social media, beneath the performative rage of BLM—indeed, beneath cancel culture itself. It is anguish. These days, many people who claim to be victims are indeed victims. But they are not victims of the oppressions and exclusions they've been taught to make central to their self-conceptions—the "gender binary", "heteronormativity", "structural racism", chimerical "phobes".

No. Like many others born after 1960, they are victims of a destructive maelstrom that rattled and shrank and sometimes destroyed their families, that undermined their churches, and that uprooted their communities. From that wreckage, identity politics sends up a howl for a world more ordered, protective, and connected than most modern humans can know. People drawn to the promise of identity politics sense that the world into which they were born is somehow inhuman. They want out.

They are not wrong in apprehending that something crucial has been somehow taken from them. They are merely mistaken about its rightful name. This, too, is not altogether their fault. Many believers have trimmed their religious sails to allow for the prevailing winds in society, meaning, ignoring the "social issues" that jeopardize standing. Many have also mocked and marginalized those who defend natural law and biblical teaching. A growing chorus says, "Capitulate". Accept that people are whoever they say they are. Celebrate the behaviors that Christianity declared off-limits for two thousand years. Put down the Bible, and pick up the cool-kid flag.

Believers exhausted by the culture wars convince themselves that surrender is "loving". Yet what if embracing people as they are, and *only* as they are, ignores their pain and fails to address that pain—and the deeper reasons for it? The torment out there is real, and it is ubiquitous. Idly reading online one day, I came across a piece about six different celebrities who had recently designated themselves "nonbinary". Within minutes of googling, something stunning emerged: every individual on that list shared two common harms—divorced or absent parents and violent childhood or adolescent abuse, in almost all cases sexual.[6]

This should make readers wonder. What if the dominant storyline about gender self-invention is all wrong?

---

[6] Mary Eberstadt, "Might Trauma Affect Gender Identity?", *Newsweek*, July 16, 2021, https://www.newsweek.com/might-trauma-affect-gender-identity-opinion-1608073. Following the appearance of that piece, a therapist emailed in confidence to say, in effect, that everyone who treats gender dysphoria knows that trauma is almost always the common denominator and that all therapists fear to say so because it would result in the revocation of their licenses.

What if the cheerleading drowns out other cries? What if childhood and adolescent trauma, combined with the radical uncertainties of family and communal life, contributes to today's gender confusion and gender migration? If that is so, then embracing transgenderism is at best iatrogenic, and at worst betrays cold-blooded indifference.

Third, proverbial cries for help are not limited to those confused about sex and gender. They abound across the United States and beyond.

Well before the pandemic, new data indicated a steep rise in psychiatric problems among American teenagers and young adults. In 2020, drug overdoses in the United States reached the highest level ever recorded in a twelve-month period. "Loneliness studies" abound, spotlighting the isolation of the elderly in every Western nation. There's an intensifying push for more euthanasia, another consequence of today's love deficit. A tsunami of pornography—about which one hears nothing from people who claim a monopoly on "social justice"—continues to destroy marriage and romance and families. As for the poor, they have always been the revolution's cannon fodder. Families frayed, unchurched, and without strong communities, they remain the hardest hit.

Within the churches, as well as outside them, resistance to naming the roots of today's plight continues. This is especially true of Christians who mock their brothers and sisters for supposed obsession with the "pelvic issues". It is past time to abandon that japery and join the countercultural activists seeking to undo some of the damage that self-styled "reformers" ignore. Rollback, not acquiescence, is what social justice and the cries of the wounded demand.

As chapters 8 through 10 indicate, the identity crisis now roiling the Western world has infiltrated the Church. What sunders Christians today is not science. It is not the desire of traditionalists to worship in Latin. It is not even the self-inflicted wounds of clerical sex scandals, grave though these are. No. The religious divide of our time is between those who think they can compromise with the sexual revolution without compromising their faith and those who are awakening to the fact that this experiment has been tried and has failed. It has failed not only institutionally, but morally. The Church of Being Nice shortchanges its victims and ignores their scars. The Church grounded on belief in redemption and a benevolent Creator must not.

In the end, the choice is simple. One either believes that there are souls on the line—including the souls of those who hate what Christianity stands for or what they think it stands for—or one does not. Christianity must witness as best it can to the truth that mankind's problem today is not with creation. It is rather with interference in that creation by an ongoing revolutionary experiment—one that sweat and prayer and grace may yet turn around.

PART III

WHAT IS THE REVOLUTION DOING TO POLITICS?

5

Two Nations, Revisited

In a landmark speech delivered in 1997, about midway between the birth of the sexual revolution and today, James Q. Wilson, one of the most eminent social scientists of the twentieth century, identified the root of America's fracturing in the dissolution of the family. Professor of government at Harvard University, professor emeritus at UCLA, and a former head of the American Political Science Association, the distinguished scholar received the American Enterprise Institute's 1997 Francis Boyer Award at the think tank's annual dinner. Wilson used the opportunity to introduce a new line of sociological argument: what he called "the two nations" of America.[1]

The image of "two nations", Wilson explained, harked back to an 1845 novel by Benjamin Disraeli, the future prime minister of Great Britain. These were the separate, nonintersecting worlds of rich and poor. Between these two nations that Disraeli described, there was "no intercourse and no sympathy"—they were "as ignorant of each other's habits, thoughts, and feelings, as if they were ... inhabitants of different planets".

[1] James Q. Wilson, "Two Nations" (lecture, American Enterprise Institute for Public Policy Research, Washington, DC, December 4, 1997), https://www.aei.org/research-products/speech/two-nations/.

More than a century and a half later, Wilson argued, the United States had also become "two nations", but the dividing line was no longer one of income or social class. Instead, it had become all about the family—specifically, whether one hailed from a broken or intact home. "It is not money", he observed, "but the family that is the foundation of public life. As it has become weaker, every structure built upon that foundation has become weaker."

Wilson called attention to what he saw as a national catastrophe in the making: the creation of generations of young men unhabituated to responsibility and protecting others. His analysis harnessed decades of recent social science that had become the mainstay of *The Public Interest*, *Commentary*, and other venues where neoconservatism sought to connect data with transformative public policy. It also joined a widening body of work on the problems famously (and infamously) identified in 1965, in Daniel Patrick Moynihan's report *The Negro Family*. By 1997, as Wilson.explained, family breakdown in America was no longer a phenomenon of the ghetto, but a national fact.

Wilson pointed above all to the many books and studies affirming correlations between home life and street life. Family structure, he demonstrated, had become more important to positive outcomes than race, income, or one's station at birth:

> Children in one-parent families, compared to those in two-parent ones, are twice as likely to drop out of school. Boys in one-parent families are much more likely than those in two-parent ones to be both out of school and out of work. Girls in one-parent families are twice as likely as those in two-parent ones to have an out-of-wedlock birth. These differences are not explained by income.... Children raised in single-parent homes [are] more likely to be suspended from school, to have emotional problems, and to behave badly.

The research overwhelmingly showed that family stability has come to trump material assets as the main currency of these two new nations. So much of this social science evidence now exists, Wilson joked, that "even some sociologists believe it."

The comment was made in jest, but it presaged our current puzzling situation. Even before 1997, evidence from all over the social sciences *already* indicated that the sexual revolution was leaving a legacy of destruction. Many more books and scholars and research studies later, a whole new wing has been added to that same library Wilson drew from, all demonstrating his point: the new wealth in America is familial wealth, and the new poverty, familial poverty.

Decades later, it is past time to ask a radical question: What has been the effect of all this social science? Has it helped to make two nations into one again? Has it ameliorated the problems that Wilson and other bold thinkers have been elucidating since the 1960s?

The answer to all three questions is no. To acknowledge this reality is not to fault the scholarship. Alongside Wilson stand other pioneering analysts across the decades who were ahead of their time, among them Midge Decter, George Gilder, Lionel Tiger, on up to contemporary trailblazers like sociologists W. Bradford Wilcox and Mark Regnerus.[2] Then as now, their work is vital. But it confronts longstanding postrevolutionary aversion to rethinking the consequences of sexual liberation. As a result, the

[2] See Midge Decter, *The New Chastity and Other Arguments against Women's Liberation* (London: Wildwood House, 1973); George Gilder, *Sexual Suicide* (Chicago IL: Quandrangle, 1973); Lionel Tiger, *The Decline of Males: The First Look at an Unexpected New World for Men and Women* (Racine, WI: Golden Books Publishing, 1999); W. Bradford Wilcox, *Why Marriage Matters: Thirty Conclusions from the Social Sciences*, 3rd ed. (New York, NY: Broadway Books, 2011); Mark Regnerus, *Cheap Sex: The Transformation of Men, Marriage, and Monogamy* (Oxford: Oxford University Press, 2017).

social problems incurred by just that continue to flourish. Consider three examples.

The first is one that no one saw coming: nationwide revelations of widespread sexual harassment, and the ensuing "#MeToo" movement.

In 2017, a few isolated reports about depravity in Hollywood went on to become a cavalcade of revelations concerning sexual predation in one high-profile industry after another. For the next several years, public attention concentrated on itinerant details of these stories—the trials of the accused, the victims, the powerful men ousted from power by accusations lobbed with wildly various standards of proof.

Yet for all the attention these immorality tales garnered in the news cycle, the most salient point they raised went largely unremarked. The sheer magnitude of the #MeToo scandals pointed to an altogether different question: What, exactly, had made these multidimensional depredations, or alleged depredations, possible in the first place?

After all, as jaded pundits remarked at the time, men behaving badly isn't exactly news. But men taking for granted the sexual availability of any given woman, in one arena after another—that *is* new. That is something that only the Pill and related technologies could have made possible. Only in a society where systemic sterility is the norm would any man dare to proposition women on the spot, over and over, as appears to have been the case in the #MeToo revelations.

In other words, no Pill, no sexual-harassment scandals on the scale seen today.

#MeToo also intersects with the post-Pill order in another, more subterranean way. The diminution of the family has not only freed women to behave as men do in the paid workplace. These gains have also been purchased against numerical losses. For starters, many men are now deprived by demographic subtraction of sisters and daughters. Many women are similarly deprived of brothers and sons. And, of course, divorce and cohabitation have also subtracted biological parents, particularly fathers, from the lives of many boys and girls.

What might be the net effect of those losses? One answer is a world in which the sexes know less about one another than they used to—in which many women no longer know any men as protectors, but only as predators. There, many men who lack sisters, cousins, and other familial feminine connections "learn" about women mainly through other means, including the lies absorbed in watching pornography.

Certainly the aggression revealed in many #MeToo accounts followed the pornographic script. Grisly details caused observers to wonder: *What's wrong with these men? Don't they have mothers, sisters, and other women in their lives? How could they act this way, if that were the case?* The answer may well be that many men today do *not* have much familial experience of the opposite sex—and many women do not, either.

More and more people also have no experience with organized religion. This new form of illiteracy has far-reaching implications for society, including for how the sexes behave toward one another—or not. Those with a religious background are instructed to treat one another as figurative sisters and brothers, united in fellowship. Thanks to the many acts of human subtraction since the 1960s, this path to social knowledge is another that seems more elusive than before.

Again, behold the irony: the revolution has rendered sex itself more ubiquitous than ever. But it has also estranged men and women as never before, both by shrinking the family and by increasing the mistrust thanks to widespread sexual consumerism. Pornography and pornography-infused dating apps like Tinder poison romance by teaching people to shop for fellow members of *Homo sapiens* with as much calculation as they shop for headphones and yoga mats. One consequence would have been unthinkable until the last couple of decades: pornography is now a major factor cited in divorces.[3]

Its lies not only make the rounds—they are *believed*, and they affect personal behavior. When a preeminent television host fell from grace following multiple accusations of what just about any woman would call predatory conduct, he said in a statement: "I always felt that I was pursuing shared feelings."[4] Awful though his conduct allegedly was, those words ring with authenticity. Many men believe similarly in the untruths that have been spreading across the human race for half a century now—beginning with the sophism that both sexes take the same view of supposedly consequence-free recreational sex.

To observe the potency of such disinformation is not to exonerate offenders. It is merely to acknowledge that mass confusion of a whole new order now plagues romance. By way of illustration, sculptor Frederick Hart's magnificent and often-photographed sculpture *Ex Nihilo*, on the front of the Washington National Cathedral, comes to mind. It depicts beautiful human bodies emerging from chaos as God creates the world. Postrevolution, romance for

[3] David Shultz, "Divorce Rates Double When People Start Watching Porn", *Science*, August 26, 2016, https://www.science.org/content/article/divorce-rates-double-when-people-start-watching-porn.

[4] Irin Carmon and Amy Brittain, "Eight Women Say Charlie Rose Sexually Harassed Them", *Washington Post*, November 20, 2017, https://www.washingtonpost.com/investigations/eight-women-say-charlie-rose-sexually-harassed-them--with-nudity-groping-and-lewd-calls/2017/11/20/9b168de8-caec-11e7-8321-481fd63f174d_story.html.

many seems the opposite of what Hart so tenderly rendered. Today, beautiful human beings do not so much arise from chaos fully formed, but instead plummet into it like Dante's Paolo and Francesca—endlessly circling, and never really touching.

Now consider three other ways in which the same social shifts destabilize today's political order.

One concerns the modern welfare state and its sustainability in the coming decades. It does not take an economist to see that welfare schemes premised on family sizes of yesteryear will collapse under today's flights from weddings and births. Also obvious, the fractured family is a major engine of the welfare state itself. Paternal government is the financial backer that makes single motherhood—and absent fatherhood—possible.

In effect, the state has become the angel investor of family dysfunction. Paternal government moves in to pick up the pieces of the shattered family—but, by bankrolling it, paternal government ensures more of the same. Economists are fond of saying that the way to ensure more of something is to subsidize it. That is exactly what the welfare state has been doing across the free societies of the West: subsidizing family breakdown. The sundering of the family has rendered modern government a flush but controlling super-daddy.

This dynamic has profound political implications.[5] Over 40 percent of children born in the United States today are born to unmarried parents.[6] Twenty years ago, that

[5] This is especially true for Americans who regard themselves as conservatives and constitutionalists first. Unless and until there is familial and religious revival, arguments on behalf of limited government are futile.

[6] Elizabeth Wildsmith, Jennifer Manlove, and Elizabeth Cook, "Dramatic Increase in the Proportion of Births Outside of Marriage in the United States from 1990 to 2016", *ChildTrends*, August 8, 2018, https://www.childtrends .org/publications/dramatic-increase-in-percentage-of-births-outside-marriage -among-whites-hispanics-and-women-with-higher-education-levels.

number was around one-third. Absent *some* form of moral or religious renaissance, the state will continue to play the role of super-daddy. In other words, no rollback of the sexual revolution, no rollback of the federal government.

A second way in which the revolution has transformed politics is just as consequential. That is the symbiotic bond between the diminution of the family and the rise of identity politics. As chapter 7, "The Fury of the Fatherless", explains in more detail, today's obsession with self is one more consequence of the postrevolutionary family deficit. Organic connections have been sundered as never before, outside wartime or natural catastrophe. We learn less in the trusted circle of the family than the people before us, because we have so many fewer people from whom to learn. Liberation from *material* nature has exacted an *immaterial* cost—a secure sense of self and place.

A third form of political fallout is more prosaic, though no less compelling. Even more than two decades ago, evidence abounds that existential suffering is the order of the day for many. Something about life in the modern West must be at the root of it.

This, too, is reflected in politics. The presidential election of 2016 was widely held to be one of the most rancorous in history—a new low for American politics. But it surely reflected even greater social discontent roiling underneath the surface. From the United States to Western Europe and beyond, citizens in the world's most materially advanced societies are feeling angry, ignored, and disenfranchised. And today, even more than in 1997, it is incontestable that politics alone will not heal their wounds.

In the United States, millions continue to look to government and to political-cultural "tribes" to replace what they have lost—connections to family and transcendent communities. Informed analyses of rural America and the opioid epidemic and the disappearance of manufacturing jobs wrestle some of this pain into prose.[7] Even so, beneath visible crises like unemployment in the Rust Belt and the opioid explosion, the fault line remains the one identified by Wilson: the family.

Globalization is part of this same crisis, of course. So is the immediacy of the internet, which shows the have-nots what the haves enjoy up close and more personal than ever before, even as it provides the angry and discontented a convening power never available until now. Even so, what most ails great swaths of the country today is something more fundamental than income disparity or a Gini coefficient, and more natural than any digital act of bonding.

James Q. Wilson's proposed answer to the postrevolutionary question was meliorative and, essentially, political. He advocated early, extensive, and expensive intervention for the youngest children at risk, based on the fact that social science had also shown those early years to be critical. Many today would cast a colder eye on the possibility of government action providing any relief. America's deepest problems spring from a more primordial place.

Being "heard", "seen", and "recognized" are not the stuff of democratic politics as usual. Nor is the despair incarnate in today's rates of substance addiction, or the related fact that psychiatrists and psychologists have been reporting for many years that mental-health trouble is on the rise, especially among women and the young. Politics

[7] See Beth Macy, *Dopesick: Dealers, Doctors, and the Drug Company That Addicted America* (New York, NY: Little, Brown and Company, 2018); Sam Quinones, *Dreamland: The True Tale of America's Opiate Epidemic* (London: Bloomsbury Publishing, 2015); and Quinones' follow-up book on the subsequent explosion of synthetic drugs, *The Least of Us: True Tales of America and Hope in the Time of Fentanyl and Meth* (London: Bloomsbury Publishing, 2021).

alone did not create these problems. That is why politics alone will not solve them, either.

The gin alleys of London gave rise to Victorian moral renewal. The rough mayhem of an earlier America spawned the Great Awakening, which continues to echo through the sturdier corridors of American Protestantism. Earlier waves of American drug addiction—cocaine, crack cocaine, crystal meth, even nicotine—are no longer focuses of great public concern because the crises passed. As Wilson noted, explaining his own optimism despite his unflinching analysis, "America has been told that it would be destroyed by slavery, alcohol, subversion, immigration, civil war, economic collapse, and atom bombs, and it has survived them all."

In November 2017, after scandals had been rolling out for weeks, the *Washington Post* published a piece that would have been unthinkable in that secular standard-bearer pre-Harvey Weinstein. "Let's Rethink Sex", by columnist Christine Emba, criticized what she called "America's prevailing and problematic sexual ethic—one that is in no small part responsible for getting us into this sexual misconduct mess in the first place".[8]

That piece was a harbinger of what has become an unmistakable new revisionism. The lessons of the #MeToo movement may yet succeed in doing what generations of clergy have not: gaining a new hearing for traditionalism, or at least a new look at anything-goes libertarianism.

Occam's razor bends toward truth. Traditionalists and other contrarians have been right to argue that the revolution would lead to rising trouble between the sexes and

---

[8] Christine Emba, "Let's Rethink Sex", *Washington Post*, November 26, 2017, https://www.washingtonpost.com/opinions/lets-rethink-sex/2017/11/26/d8546a86-d2d5-11e7-b62d-d9345ced896d_story.html.

a decline in respect for women—just as James Q. Wilson remains right that family and lack of family have replaced money itself as the nation's most accurate measures of real wealth and poverty.

Future decades will show whether the secular sex scandals of 2017 and 2018 amount to a passing news drama, or instead an actual turning point in society's understanding of itself. Meanwhile, the empirical record remains even clearer now than it was twenty years ago—and it will still be clear twenty, or for that matter two hundred, years from now, whether generations practiced in denial acknowledge as much.

6

How the Family Gap Undercuts
Western Freedom

The notion that Hugh Hefner's America has exacted political costs, including rising economic costs, might sound novel. Yet examples offered in the preceding chapter are just the beginning. Another repercussion is just as fundamental, and it appears with increasing frequency in the courts. It arises because the liberationist agenda remains on a collision course with essential teachings of Christianity. The longer that agenda is written into law, the more religious freedom is at risk.

Consider a snapshot. In a speech to the Federalist Society in November 2020, Supreme Court Justice Samuel A. Alito Jr. reiterated his concern that "in certain quarters, religious liberty is fast becoming a disfavored right."[1] Small wonder that the subject was on his mind. A week earlier, the court had heard oral arguments in one more seminal religious liberty case, *Fulton v. City of Philadelphia*. In it, Catholic Social Services (CSS)—one of some thirty agencies used by the city to place foster children in private homes—claimed religious exemption for its policy of placing kids in traditional mom-and-dad family settings.

[1] Samuel A. Alito Jr. (keynote address, National Lawyer's Convention, Federalist Society, November 12, 2020), https://www.rev.com/blog/transcripts/supreme-court-justice-samuel-alito-speech-transcript-to-federalist-society.

So far, one might think, so unremarkable: a Catholic agency conforms its good works to Catholic principles. But what about nontraditional couples, like those of the same sex? As it happens, CSS was not approached by any such couples looking for kids—likely because all the other thirty agencies remained available to them. In fact, CSS would even refer same-sex couples to those other agencies, if needed. Thus far, at least, Philadelphia seems to have enjoyed a live-and-let-live solution to a pluralist polity in which diverse points of view coexist. No one appears to have suffered from CSS's policies, and children in need of loving homes seem to have been helped.

So why did Philadelphia stop referring foster children to CSS, thus prompting the suit that put this case before the court? As Justice Alito observed: "If we are honest about what's really going on here, it's not about ensuring that same-sex couples in Philadelphia have the opportunity to be foster parents. It's the fact [that] the city can't stand the message that Catholic Social Services and the arch-diocese are sending by continuing to adhere to the old-fashioned view about marriage."[2] Justice Brett Kavanaugh, too, remarked upon the ideological aggression of CSS's adversaries; Philadelphia, he remarked, was "looking for a fight" in ceasing its referrals.

In 2021, the court delivered a unanimous judgment, ruling that the city's refusal to provide the contract violated the Free Exercise Clause. Though a victory for religious freedom, the case was also of limited consolation; the grounds on which it was decided were so narrow as

[2] Michael Foust, "Supreme Court Appears Poised to Side with Religious Liberty in LGBT Adoption Case", *Christian Headlines*, November 5, 2020, https://www.christianheadlines.com/contributors/michael-foust/supreme -court-appears-poised-to-side-with-religious-liberty-in-lgbt-adoption-case .html.

to disquiet partisans on both sides who were hoping for a more definitive verdict.[3]

Even so, the significance of this particular dispute transcends the ruling. The Philadelphia case joins a growing list in which do-gooding by people known as Christians has been punished with financially and otherwise draining lawsuits—even when, as in *Fulton v. City of Philadelphia*, the harm to anyone is nonexistent. Thus the Little Sisters of the Poor have been dragged through the courts for years, deposed and otherwise menaced, even though their alleged social crime—objecting to being forced to provide contraception—has not impeded one soul, then or now, from locating all manner of such devices everywhere in the United States. Masterpiece Cakes in Colorado was hounded for refusing to participate in same-sex weddings—even though the antagonistic party was never at risk of lacking wedding cake or anything nuptial at all, following *Obergefell v. Hodges*.

Such cases ignite the suspicion that people are being targeted for suits and harassed in courts *because* they are believing Christians. As Rod Dreher summarizes, "[A] progressive—and profoundly anti-Christian—militancy is steadily overtaking society.... [It] takes material form in government and private institutions, in corporations, in academia and media, and in the changing practices of everyday American life.... There is virtually nowhere left to hide."[4]

Dreher and others focus naturally on what this new animus is doing to the faithful. Just as crucial is another

[3] See Madeline Carlisle and Belinda Luscombe, "Supreme Court Sides with Catholic Agency in LGBTQ Foster Care Case—But Avoids Major Religious Freedom Questions", *Time*, June 17, 2021, https://time.com/6074119/supreme-court-foster-care-ruling-fulton-philadelphia/.

[4] Rod Dreher, *Live Not by Lies: A Manual for Christian Dissidents* (New York, NY: Sentinel 2020), xiii.

question that will also shape Christianity's future in America, and for that matter, everyone else's: Where is this new animus coming from?

After all, it is not as if social conservatism or religious traditionalism directs today's cultural traffic. Same-sex marriage has been legal in the United States since 2015. Transgender actors, athletes, celebrities, influencers, models, and beauty pageant contestants have become as ubiquitous as Disney trademarks. The Gramscian march through institutions has been nowhere as successful as in the public school system, where sex-first "sexual education" curricula from kindergarten onward has been entrenched for years, and where parents are only beginning to question the progressive tide. Meanwhile, for all the affrighted talk of subservient "handmaids", abortion on demand continues its bloody gallop along.

Hollywood, Silicon Valley, and almost every humanities faculty in the land are thoroughly repaganized. So are the human resources departments and workplace mores of many American corporations. So, especially, is Big Tech. And with a few exceptions, the churches remain in crouch mode. Riven by long-running civil wars over the sexual revolution, they are nowhere playing offense in this great scramble over who owns the cultural real estate of the Western future.

So what continues to goad the people who cannot live and let live in the matter of Christianity?

Pedestrian, entrenched bureaucracy is one culprit. Like Teddy Brewster in *Arsenic and Old Lace*, who does not understand that the battle for San Juan Hill has been over for some time, today's alphabet activists continue charging ... *somewhere*. And so the victorious advocates for same-sex marriage, far from packing up and going home all these years after *Obergefell*, expand their political portfolios with new demands—such as that accreditation be removed from Christian schools or that biological boys be forced onto sports teams for biological girls. This kind of bureaucratic bloating is the fruit of something prosaic known as "mission creep".

A more systemic answer to the question of today's animus against Christianity is also in order. The American family, as revisited, has changed radically during the past sixty years. Less than one-fifth of households now conform to the "nuclear family" model of mother, father, and children. In 1960, that number was 45 percent.[5] The family has also shrunk. Reiterating a crucial point made earlier on, children today are considerably less likely to have siblings—and by extension, cousins, aunts, and uncles—than they were sixty years ago. Almost 30 percent of all households consist of just one person. Some 40 percent of all children lack a biological father in the home.

Such momentous, ubiquitous changes to kinship have had, and continue to have, momentous and ubiquitous consequences. How could they not? A world of fewer and weaker family ties is one in which deprived people are furious about things they do not have or no longer know.

Exhibit A is the seemingly bizarre outpouring on the left that greeted the nomination of Justice Amy Coney Barrett to the Supreme Court. "An anti-choice fanatic with seven kids", ran a typical slur.[6] Her confirmation hearing was "child-obsessed" and used "children as talking points", showcasing Barrett's "prolific motherhood", complained

[5] Eric Schmidt, "For First Time, Nuclear Families Drop Below 25 Percent of Households", *New York Times*, May 15, 2001, https://www.nytimes.com/2001/05/15/us/for-first-time-nuclear-families-drop-below-25-of-households.html.

[6] Amanda Marcotte, "Why Are Republicans Obsessed with Amy Coney Barrett's Kids? To Troll Feminists", *Salon*, October 13, 2020, https://www.salon.com/2020/10/13/why-are-republicans-obsessed-with-amy-coney-barretts-kids-to-troll-feminists/.

the *Washington Post*.[7] Activists for the new racialism, including Ibram X. Kendi, director of the recently created Boston University Center for Antiracist Research, cast ugly aspersions on the fact that two of the Barretts' children had been adopted from Haiti.[8] Beneath the ultimately ineffectual sniping, the collective gasp was practically audible. *Seven kids? Who does that?*

Once again, the point is inescapable: postrevolutionary practices mean that access to some basic human goods has become problematic. By now, for example, generations of American women have been raised to fear their own fertility, and to see life as a zero-sum game in which babies equal career cancellation. By dint of her mere example, Justice Barrett gave those people the shock of their lives. And by raising, however tacitly, the forbidden thought that families and professional accomplishment might be workable together after all, her example no doubt set off other unwanted notions, long suppressed—including about families and their preeminence, period.

The ire directed at the Barretts inadvertently revealed two deeper currents of today's rough social seas. First, many Americans, especially on the progressive side, are now ignorant of what was, until yesterday, an elementary reality—that there are intact families with more than one or two children. Second, woke women, in particular, can be moved to fury at the sight of a mother with husband

---

[7] Robin Givhan, "Supreme Court Nominee Amy Coney Barrett Has Seven Kids. And Don't You Dare Forget It", *Washington Post*, October 12, 2020, https://www.washingtonpost.com/nation/2020/10/12/supreme-court -nominee-amy-coney-barrett-has-seven-kids-dont-you-dare-forget-it/.

[8] "Some White colonizers 'adopted' Black children. They 'civilized' these 'savage' children in the 'superior' ways of White people, while using them as props in their lifelong pictures of denial, while cutting the biological parents of these children out of the picture of humanity." Ibram X. Kendi (@DrIbram), Twitter, September 26, 2020, https://twitter.com/dribram/status/1309916696 296198146?lang=en. This tweet was later deleted by Kendi.

and several children. This returns us to the deficits incurred by the revolution and its spurious promises. What is fury, but the flip side of loss?

Consider a second example of how the hunger for connections once supplied by family deforms politics: the BLM-driven protests and riots that roiled cities across the country throughout 2020. The following chapter, "The Fury of the Fatherless", examines these phenomena in detail; a few preliminary observations here about the links between familial disorder and social disorder can help to set the stage.

Who, for starters, has the wherewithal to attend protests night after night for months on end, as has happened for years in Portland, Oregon? For the most part, not people living in families, and certainly not mothers and fathers caring for young children.

Biographies of some of the actors involved in particular tragedies emphasize the point. Consider the profile of the shootings in Kenosha, Wisconsin, during a demonstration on August 25. The shooter, seventeen-year-old Kyle Rittenhouse, lived with his single mother.[9] At least two of the three men who were shot, and who were regulars at the downtown protests, were children of broken homes.[10] Two of the protesters also had children of their own and were not married. And so on. Such biographical strands lace other stories of disengaged young men with disproportionate attractions to groups that operate as

[9] Jemima McEvoy, "Kyle Rittenhouse's Mother Says Her Son Shouldn't Have Been in Kenosha", *Forbes*, November 10, 2020, https://www.forbes.com/sites/jemimamcevoy/2020/11/10/kyle-rittenhouses-mother-says-her-son-shouldnt-have-been-in-kenosha/?sh=37c96c2f650a.

[10] Vanessa Romo and Sharon Pruitt-Young, "What We Know about the 3 Men Who Were Shot by Kyle Rittenhouse", *NPR*, November 20, 2021, https://www.npr.org/2021/11/20/1057571558/what-we-know-3-men-kyle-rittenhouse-victims-rosenbaum-huber-grosskreutz.

family substitutes—whether street gangs, BLM, or other identitarian groups, right and left alike.

Consider a case from 2019 in Eugene, Oregon.[11] There, a young man, in the midst of a custody dispute, was shot and killed by police at his daughter's middle school. He was carrying a gun and had an extra clip in his belt. A veteran, he was divorced from his wife, after which he became involved with a series of activist groups on and off his college campus. These included Latino and LGBTQ organizations, as well as a community for self-defense that trained people in firearm use. By the end of his short life, this prospective shooter was also using the pronouns "they/them" to refer to himself.

His tragic story could be interpreted variously as a cautionary tale about trauma in wartime, or about the deadly ease of obtaining firearms, or about police bias against sexual minorities, or about some other politically spun topic of the day. But surely its primordial caption would be: *This man suffered a radical severing from his family, followed by identity dissolution that ended in violence and death.*

That familial loss had something to do with the 2020 protests is also revealed by some of BLM's theatrics: shining flashlights into private homes, waking families by screaming in the middle of the night, and disrupting outdoor meals. This last misanthropic stroke has by now a substantial history among left-wing activists in the United States. #BlackBrunch, a similar set of movements that has also aggressively interrupted diners in cities around the country, began in Oakland, California, in 2015.[12] The stated

[11] Christian Hill, "Love and Rage", *Register-Guard*, March 14, 2019, https://stories.usatodaynetwork.com/landeros/home/.

[12] Lee Romney, "#BlackBrunch Brings Peaceful Protest to Oakland Restaurants", *Los Angeles Times*, January 4, 2015, https://www.latimes.com/local/california/la-me-black-brunch-20150105-story.html.

purpose of these intrusions is to invade "traditionally white spaces" to raise awareness of black suffering.

But what is specifically "white" about dining out? More telling is *what* is being disrupted here. People dine out with family and friends—their smallest and dearest communities. In the rage caught on videos throughout summer 2020, another possibility for the origin of these disruptions emerges: resentment of those who do enjoy their social and familial ties. Why else would anyone exult in upending one of life's universal pleasures: time alone in a relaxed setting with loved ones and friends?

As the phrase "protest families" signals, other details also suggest that some of the discontent out there has familial roots. It was reported from Portland during summer 2020, for example, that protesters taunted cops with the chant "Your children will hate you."[13] What kind of political statement is that, if not one of rage against people who *do* have families? Similarly, across the United States, furious mobs toppled monuments of past leaders—not just those of Confederates, but of anything that looked like a male authority figure, including, in Washington, D.C., one of Mahatma Gandhi. Tearing down a Confederate statue is a political statement. Tearing down statues of men indiscriminately is a daddy issue.

And it is here that the family-deprived, untethered mobs of 2020 intersect indelibly with the new animus against Christianity. For 2020 was not only remarkable on account of BLM and other unrest in the streets. The discontent brought with it a stunning rise in attacks on churches and other religious structures across the country, as the United

[13] Douglas Murray, "My Week with the Baying Antifa Mob", *Spectator*, October 24, 2020, https://www.spectator.co.uk/article/my-week-with-the-baying-antifa-mob.

States Conference of Catholic Bishops summarized in a press release expressing the alarm at this increase in vandalism and desecrations.[14]

At least thirty-seven incidents occurred across twenty states after June 22 of that year. The cause of one, the fire at Mission San Gabriel Arcángel in the Archdiocese of Los Angeles, is still unknown. Incidents include arson; statues beheaded, dismembered, smashed, and painted; gravestones defaced with swastikas and anti-Catholic language and American flags next to them burned; and other examples of destruction and vandalism. The full list of particulars ran to six and a half closely spaced pages. Similarly, both the leak of the Supreme Court's *Dobbs* draft and the release of the decision itself were followed by spates of desecration and vandalism, aimed first and foremost at Catholic properties. All of which raises the question: Why churches?

After all, if the protests were about racism, it is hard to see the benefit of attacking houses of worship—especially the Catholic Church, some of whose clergy were on the front lines of the civil rights movement, whose schools in the inner city and elsewhere have been among the surest tickets to a better life for generations, and whose global hierarchy and laity include representatives of every shade of melanin known to nature.

The answer can only be that, as the most visible remaining defenders of the traditional family, the churches are natural lightning rods for the anger and the woe that a social order deprived of robust family ties invariably produces. Again, the clash between the uncompromising

---

[14] United States Conference of Catholic Bishops, "One Hundred Incidents of Vandalism Reported at Catholic Sites in U.S. Since May 2020", news release, October 14, 2021, https://www.usccb.org/news/2021/one-hundred -incidents-vandalism-reported-catholic-sites-us-may-2020.

religious belligerency of secularism, on the one hand, and the religious liberty guaranteed by constitutional republics, on the other, looks to have become a perpetual conflict.

Denial of the fact America is ailing because its families are ailing springs eternal, of course.[15] In a piece for the *Atlantic* published in 2021, announcing that "The Nuclear Family Was a Mistake", *New York Times* columnist David Brooks acknowledges in passing that America's kinship implosion has unleashed "an epidemic of trauma", especially among the worse-off.[16] Even so, he argues, the time has come to drop the illusion that Mom, Pop, and the kids could ever be all right. Hoping to put the culture wars behind, he lauds the vogue for "chosen families", meaning "the rise of new living arrangements that bring nonbiological kin into family or family-like relationships".

Such artificially forged familial identities might be attractive to adults practiced in consumerism. But their appeal eludes the most vulnerable members of society—children and old people, say. The notion that boys or girls thrive around males to whom they are not biologically related is overruled by generations of social science about the risks of just that. As the *New York Times* put it, summarizing a representative study published in *Pediatrics*, "Living with an unrelated adult, especially an unrelated man, substantially increases the risk that a child will die violently.... [C]hildren who live with adults who are not biologically related to them are nearly 50 times as likely to die at the adults' hands as children who live with two biological parents, the

---

[15] I described this reflex as "rounding the bases of denial, heated denial, and damned denial", *Adam and Eve after the Pill* (San Francisco: Ignatius Press, 2012), 23.

[16] David Brooks, "The Nuclear Family Was a Mistake", *Atlantic*, March 2020, https://www.theatlantic.com/magazine/archive/2020/03/the-nuclear-family-was-a-mistake/605536/.

researchers said."[17] Similar findings summarize the perils to some elderly of institutional care.[18] And beyond such empirical cautions lie matters of the heart. What child or great-grandparent, given the choice, would prefer a "chosen family" to one of his very own?

"Chosen families", like street gangs, are mothered by the necessity of human nature. If families cannot exist, their simulacra must be invented. That is why strained substitutes for kin have proliferated across the decades since the sexual revolution took off. All are part of the ongoing, post-1960s transfer of social capital, according to which more and more of it accrues to the strongest members of society, leaving the weakest even more vulnerable than before.

This brings us to the grittiest truth not only of 2020, but of the future it foretells. A consequential subset of America now roams the nation and the internet in search of family substitutes: street gangs, "chosens", identitarian groups, BLM, and toxic ideologies. None of these alternatives is remotely up to the job done by the functioning real thing—or even the semifunctioning real thing. To paraphrase James Q. Wilson's point in chapter 5, the new American "haves" are those who have managed, through luck or hard work or both, to maintain vigorous family ties despite it all. The new have-nots are those who suffer

---

[17] Nicholas Bakalar, "Unrelated Adults at Home Increase Risk for Children", *New York Times*, November 8, 2005, https://www.nytimes.com/2005/11/08/health/unrelated-adults-at-home-increase-risk-for-children.html.

[18] For example, one meta-analysis of nine studies on elder abuse in institutional settings found that "64.2 percent of staff admitted to elder abuse in the past year" and concluded that "the prevalence of elder abuse in institutions is high." Yongfie Yon, Maria Ramiro-Gonzalez, Christopher R. Mikton, Manfred Huber, and Dinesh Sethi, "The Prevalence of Elder Abuse in Institutional Settings: A Systematic Review and Meta-Analysis", *European Journal of Public Health* 29, no. 1 (February 1, 2019): 58–67, https://europepmc.org/article/PMC/PMC6359898.

from these primal losses, and who latch with increasing desperation on to collective, victim-centered "identities".

Of course the fact that the sexual revolution is uniquely responsible for what ails America and the West is not to say that it is *all* that ails America and the West. Unwitting accomplices, including social media, abound. Another and less obvious culprit is the widening ignorance of what is taught in the Good Book. As a result, people who do not believe in sin and vice no longer recognize such classics as anger and envy and pride, even as they parade across screens and streets 24/7, and even as peaceful protests turn brutal, avaricious, exhibitionist, or all three. In an age that is increasingly illiterate about all things Christian, and that no longer believes in sins, deadly or otherwise, capital vices may go unnoticed—or at least unnamed.

Yet whether spiritual or familial in origin, or both, the afflictions of the increasingly disconnected go chronically misdiagnosed. The trouble is that the excuse of myopia does not make the elemental deficits in post-1960s America any less explicable or any less destructive—or any less of a tragedy.

7

The Fury of the Fatherless

To understand how individual loss leads to collective expression, consider an excursion into a seminal event of 2020.

Beginning in May of that year, protests over the death of George Floyd in Minneapolis, Minnesota, roiled cities across the United States and throughout that summer.[1] These morphed in some cases into irrationalism, and, in some cities, extensive theft and violence. It is true that most protests were peaceful. It is also true that the exceptions, marked by violence, biliousness, unreason, and anarchy, were far more common than was understood at the time.

According to the first thorough examination of the street protests, undertaken by Armed Conflict Location and Event Data Project in conjunction with the Bridging Divides Initiative at Princeton, more than 10,600 incidents of what is benignly called "unrest" were recorded between May 24 and August 22, 2020.[2] Of these, some 570 involved

---

[1] "How George Floyd Died, and What Happened Next", *New York Times*, May 19, 2022, https://www.nytimes.com/article/george-floyd.html.

[2] Roudabeh Kishi and Sam Jones, *Demonstrations and Political Violence in America: New Data for Summer 2020*, Armed Conflict Location & Event Data Project, September 2020, https://acleddata.com/acleddatanew/wp-content/uploads/2020/09/ACLED_USDataReview_Sum2020_SeptWebPDF_HiRes.pdf.

violence. Of those, most involved Black Lives Matter (BLM) activists. Preliminary insurance estimates suggested that the damage surpassed the $1.2 billion in damages accrued during the 1992 Rodney King riots; some forecast that they ran as high as $2 billion, making these the most expensive insurance tolls of any violent demonstrations in recent history.[3] Also distinguishing these demonstrations were the atmospherics: lusty screaming, ecstatic vandalism, and the overt menacing of bystanders.

This ritualistic exhibition of destructive behaviors in city after city is without precedent in the United States. Neither footage of the civil rights demonstrations nor that of protests against the War in Vietnam looked remotely similar. The differences demand explanation. Pundits invoked the usual bête noirs: former president Donald Trump, cancel culture, police brutality, political tribalism, the coronavirus pandemic. These factors did indeed feed the "demand" side of the protests and rioting—the *reasons* for the ritualistic enactment. But what about the "supply" side: the ready and apparently inexhaustible ranks of demonstrators themselves? What explains *them*?

The answer "racism" fails to explain the aspects of this "summer of rage", which had nothing to do with police brutality and everything to do with looting, violence, and wanton destruction of property, including indiscriminate defacing and toppling of statues representing male authority figures of all kinds. The spectacle of often-white protesters screaming and throwing objects at brown and black policemen contradict anything dreamed of by critical race theory. So do the actual statistics concerning crime and

[3] Ryan Smith, "Insurance Costs for George Floyd Riots Will Be Most Expensive in History", *Insurance Business Magazine*, September 18, 2020, https://www.insurancebusinessmag.com/us/news/breaking-news/insurance-costs-for-george-floyd-riots-will-be-most-expensive-in-history-233905.aspx.

race crime.[4] So do public attitudes. In 2017, according to Pew Research, 52 percent of respondents said that race "doesn't make much difference" in marriage, and another 39 percent said that interracial marriage is "a good thing".[5] When 91 percent of the public shrugs at or applauds interracial marriage, it is absurd to speak of a spectral racism that irredeemably poisons society.

Enter a more explanatory theory: The explosive events of 2020 were but the latest eruption along a fault line running through our already unstable lives. That eruption exposes the threefold crisis of filial attachment that has beset the Western world for more than half a century. Deprived of father, Father, and *patria*, a critical mass of mankind has become dysfunctional on a scale not seen before.

This is especially true of the young. The frantic flight to collective political identities has primordial, not transient, origins. The riots were, in part, a visible consequence of the largely invisible crisis of Western paternity. Consider the variety of evidence.

First, a syllogism: The riots amounted to social dysfunction on parade. Six decades of social science have

[4] According to a database established by the *Washington Post* for the years 2015–2022, for example, roughly a thousand people in the United States are killed per year by police acting in the line of duty. Black fatalities account for around 23 percent of that total, while black Americans are 13 percent of the population. Those killed by police are overwhelmingly male and between the ages of twenty and forty. Only 15 percent of those killed in 2021 were unarmed; the rest had guns, knives, other weapons, or some combination of the three. Any loss of innocent life is tragic. The statistics, for their part, do not support the popular storyline according to which black people are overwhelmingly targeted by law enforcement for being black. See "Fatal Force", *Washington Post*, https://www.washingtonpost.com/graphics/investigations/police-shootings-database/.

[5] Gretchen Livingston and Anna Brown, "Intermarriage in the U.S. 50 Years after Loving v. Virginia", *Pew Research Center*, May 18, 2017, https://www.pewresearch.org/social-trends/2017/05/18/intermarriage-in-the-u-s-50-years-after-loving-v-virginia/.

established that the most efficient way to increase dysfunction is to increase fatherlessness. And this the United States has done, for generations now. Almost one in four children today grows up without a father in the home. For African Americans, it is some 65 percent of children.

Some people, mainly on the political left, think there is nothing to see here. They are wrong. The vast majority of incarcerated juveniles have grown up in fatherless homes.[6] Teen and other mass murderers almost invariably have filial rupture in their biographies.[7] Absent fathers predict higher rates of truancy, psychiatric problems, criminality, promiscuity, drug use, rape, domestic violence, and other tragic outcomes.[8]

Enter another pertinent, albeit socially radioactive fact: fatherlessness leads to a search for substitutes. And some of these daddy placeholders turn out to be toxic.

The murder rates in inner cities, for example, are irreducibly *familial* phenomena. That's because the murder problem is largely a gang problem, and the gang problem is largely a daddy problem. As the Minnesota Psychological Association put it in a study published in 2013:

A high percentage of gang members come from father-absent homes ... possibly resulting from a need for a

[6] See R. L. Maginnis, "Single-Parent Families Cause Juvenile Crime", *Office of Justice Programs, U.S. Department of Justice,* 1997, https://www.ojp.gov/ncjrs /virtual-library/abstracts/single-parent-families-cause-juvenile-crime-juvenile -crime-opposing. The first sentence of the abstract reads: "The *Journal of Research in Crime and Delinquency* reports that the most reliable indicator of violent crime in a community is the proportion of fatherless families."

[7] See Mary Eberstadt, *Home-Alone America: The Hidden Toll of Day Care, Behavioral Drugs, and Other Parent Substitutes* (New York, NY: Sentinel, 2004), chap. 2, "The Furious Child Problem".

[8] See, for example, the data and sources available at fathers.com concerning the correlations between fatherlessness and the behaviors enumerated.

sense of belonging. Gaining that sense of belonging is an important element for all individuals. Through gangs, youth find a sense of community and acceptance. In addition, the gang leader may fill the role of father, often leading members to model their behaviors after that individual .... Having a father in the child's life greatly reduces the likelihood of a child joining a gang.[9]

Second, the language of BLM itself suggests that paternal issues are an ingredient in the political mix that exploded in 2020 in cities across the country. Before it was removed in September of that year, one section of the BLM website declared: "We disrupt the Western-prescribed nuclear family structure requirement by supporting each other as extended families and 'villages' that collectively care for one another, especially our children, to the degree that mothers, parents, and children are comfortable."

Note the missing noun: *fathers*. It is as if fathers—as distinct from "parents"—have ceased to exist. And indeed, for at least some of the people drawn to BLM's ideology, fathers *have* ceased to exist. In this sense, BLM is a direct heir of the founding document of identity politics, the *Combahee River Collective Statement* put forward by black feminists in 1977.[10] That manifesto spoke of women and children only—never of fathers, brothers, or sons.

What does it tell us that these seminal declarations of identity politics are shot through with "the presence of the absence" of fathers? At minimum, that the politics

[9] Jerrod Brown, "Father-Absent Homes: Implications for Criminal Justice and Mental Health Professionals", *Minnesota Psychological Association*, August 2013, https://www.mnpsych.org/index.php%3Foption%3Dcom_dailyplanet blog%26view%3Dentry%26category%3Dindustry%2520news%26id%3D54.

[10] Combahee River Collective, *The Combahee River Collective Statement*, April 1977, Yale University, https://americanstudies.yale.edu/sites/default /files/files/Keyword%20Coalition_Readings.pdf.

of identity are not operating in isolation from the disappearance of paternal authority.

Third, the biographies of at least some of today's race-minded trailblazers suggest a connection between fatherlessness and identity politics. The author of the bestseller *White Fragility: Why It's So Hard for White People to Talk About Racism* was a child of divorce at age two.[11] The author of the bestseller *So You Want to Talk About Race* (2018) reports that her father left the family and broke off contact, also when she was two.[12] The author of another 2017 bestseller, *Why I'm No Longer Talking to White People about Race*, was also left by her father when very young and was raised by her single mother.[13] The author of a 2020 race book, *The Anti-Racist: How to Start a Conversation About Race and Take Action*, was raised by his grandmothers.[14] Progressive trendsetter and athlete Colin Kaepernick is another example. His biological father left his mother before he was born, and he was adopted and raised by a white family.[15] James Baldwin, a major inspiration for today's new racialist writers, grew up with an

[11] Robin DiAngelo, "My Class Didn't Trump My Race: Using Oppression to Face Privilege", *Multicultural Perspectives* 8, no. 1 (2006): 51–56.

[12] Iljeoma Oluo, "How Teju Cole Helped Me Make Peace with the Nigerian Scam Artist: Iljeoma Oluo on Reconciling Her Nigerian-American Identity", *Literary Hub*, April 15, 2016, https://lithub.com/how-teju-cole-helped-me-make-peace-with-the-nigerian-scam-artist/.

[13] Stephanie Bunbury, "Reni Eddo-Lodge and the Question of Structural Racism", *Sydney Morning Herald*, July 25, 2017, https://www.smh.com.au/entertainment/books/reni-eddolodge-and-the-question-of-structural-racism-20170724-gxhcb4.html.

[14] Brittany Britto, "Kondwani Fidel Opens Up about His Viral Essay and Giving a Voice to Black Experiences in Baltimore", *Baltimore Sun*, September 1, 2017, https://www.baltimoresun.com/features/baltimore-insider/bs-fe-kondwani-fidel-20170825-story.html.

[15] Lilyanne Rice, "Colin Kaepernick's Biological Parents—He Refuses to Meet His Biological Mother", *People*, November 5, 2021, *TheNetline*, https://thenetline.com/colin-kaepernicks-biological-parents/.

abusive stepfather and never knew his biological father; his mother left his father before he was born.[16] This list could go on.

So what? a skeptic might say. *Maybe family breakup is just part of many peoples' kitchen wallpaper by now.* True. But it may also be motivating the formation of identitarian political groups that operate as functioning families do, by providing protection and community—just as family breakup lures many fatherless kids to gangs.

Biographies on the alt-right and far-right offer similar suggestive evidence. The founder of the white nationalist group Identity Evropa is a child of divorce.[17] The neo-Nazi who founded the alt-right media network The Right Stuff is a child of divorce.[18] George Lincoln Rockwell, founder of the American Nazi Party, was a child of divorce.[19] Timothy McVeigh, the poster boy and prototype for today's violent far-right aspirants, was a child of divorce who was raised largely by his father.[20] This list, too, could go on. An *Atlantic* profile of neo-Nazi Andrew Anglin concluded: "Like so many emotionally damaged young men, [he] had

---

[16] Hilton Als, "The Enemy Within: The Making and Unmaking of James Baldwin", *New Yorker*, February 9, 1998, https://www.newyorker.com/magazine/1998/02/16/the-enemy-within-hilton-als.

[17] Gabriel Thompson, "My Brother, the White Nationalist", *Pacific Standard*, March 27, 2018, updated November 26, 2018, https://psmag.com/magazine/the-red-pill-my-brother-the-white-nationalist.

[18] Luke O'Brien, "The Making of an American Nazi", *Atlantic*, December 2017, https://www.theatlantic.com/magazine/archive/2017/12/the-making-of-an-american-nazi/544119/.

[19] Michael E. Miller, "The Shadow of an Assassinated American Nazi Commander Hangs over Charlottesville", *Washington Post*, August 21, 2017, https://www.washingtonpost.com/news/retropolis/wp/2017/08/21/the-shadow-of-an-assassinated-american-nazi-commander-hangs-over-charlottesville/.

[20] "Terror on Trial: Who Was Timothy McVeigh?", *CNN*, 2001, https://edition.cnn.com/2007/US/law/12/17/court.archive.mcveigh2/index.html?iref=nextin.

chosen to be someone, or something, bigger than himself on the internet, something ferocious to cover up the frailty he couldn't abide in himself."[21] Exactly.

Consider a fourth proof that AWOL fathers have something to do with the summer 2020 social crackup: the experimental particulars of Portland, Oregon. The city that was ground zero of nonstop protests and riots in 2020 is not just any American town. For more than thirty years, abandoned children and runaways have been a unique part of the Rose City's culture. And, for more than thirty years, documentaries and other reports on these lost children have abounded. It was Portland's permissive approach to runaways that created the nation's best-known subculture of "teen hobos", "teen homeless", and "street teens". In Portland, the link between dysfunctional kids and absent authority figures has been clear for generations now. As one researcher summarized: "The inability to emotionally connect with parents is a thread of commonality linking the narrative of street kids and travelers in Portland."[22]

Lacking family ties, Portland's feral children have bonded since the 1980s in "street families", complete with "street moms" and "street dads".[23] Some of the most grotesque crimes in the city's history have ensued thanks to

[21] O'Brien, "American Nazi".

[22] Elizabeth deLise, "Situating Street Kids: An Ethnography of Nomadic Street Kids in Portland, Oregon", *Anthropology Department Honors Papers* (New London, CT: Digital Commons @ Connecticut College, 2013), 37, https://digitalcommons.conncoll.edu/cgi/viewcontent.cgi?referer=&httpsredir=1&article=1004&context=anthrohp.

[23] See, for example, Helaine Olen, "Taking It to the Streets: Rene Denfeld, Author of a New Book on the Violent Subculture of Street Families, Talks about Why These Young Nomads Are Every Bit as Dangerous as the Bloods and the Crips", *Salon*, February 12, 2007, https://www.salon.com/2007/02/12/street_families/.

"laws" about "family" loyalty—including in 2019, when a group of three boys from such a "family" shot and killed a man as he was collecting cans, then took his car on a joyride.[24] "Street families" are an especially toxic variant of that voguish phrase encountered earlier, "chosen families". Street families are chosen families for America's broken kids. "Street families" are like other gangs: poor and desperate substitutes for the real thing, called into being by the absence of the real thing.

In the thuggish Neverland that is a part of downtown Portland, the lived connection between social breakdown and family breakdown has been inescapable since long before the death of George Floyd.

But the story of the long, hot summer of 2020 is even more complex than the subplot revolving around missing dads. As noted throughout this book, more and more Americans, especially young Americans, have suffered not one but several ruptured connections to authority and community simultaneously. That truth illuminates something otherwise opaque: why even the young who *do* come from intact homes are affected to some degree by the crisis of Western paternity.

The institutions that once anchored teenagers and young adults in paternal authority are in free fall. Their concomitant collapses generate a social anxiety that is contagious. This dynamic renders another spectacle from 2020—well-off protesters from unbroken homes smashing people's property—more intelligible than it first appears. The ubiquitous slogan in summer 2020 "People, not

[24] Shane Dixon Kavanaugh, "Portland Teens Killed Neighborhood Can Collector over Car, then Drove It to Taco Bell, Court Documents Allege", *Oregonian*, October 25, 2019, https://www.oregonlive.com/crime/2019/10 /teens-kill-neighborhood-can-collector-over-car-court-documents-allege .html.

property" inadvertently points to what ails young America most: a people deficit.

Christianity, to name one institution that bound generations to one another, began a stark decline around 1963. That decline has accelerated with particular speed among the young. In 2019, 40 percent of Americans aged eighteen to twenty-nine were "nones".[25] "None of the above" is now the fastest-growing religious subset in the United States.

There is abundant evidence that the loosening of family ties and the loosening of religious ties are linked—including among practitioners of identity politics. A 2016 study of white nationalists by the University of Virginia's Family Policies Institute, updated in 2018, turned up at least two suggestive findings. One was that subjects were much more likely to be divorced than to be married or never married.[26] Once again, family rupture and extremist identity politics connect.

The same study also confirmed that those drawn to white nationalism are unlikely to attend church (indeed, most white nationalists vehemently reject both Christianity and Judaism). Thus, religious rupture and extremist identity politics also appear to be related. The same seems true of BLM, which as a Marxist movement opposes Christianity in principle. Antifa's foot soldiers are also unlikely to tithe or spend Sunday mornings with a hymnal. This does not mean that these activists are without purpose—quite the opposite; as chapter 3 explained, the

---

[25] "In U.S., Decline of Christianity Continues at Rapid Pace", *Pew Research Center*, October 17, 2019, https://www.pewresearch.org/religion/2019/10/17/in-u-s-decline-of-christianity-continues-at-rapid-pace/.

[26] George Hawley, "The Demography of the Alt-Right", *Institute for Family Studies*, August 9, 2018, https://ifstudies.org/blog/the-demography-of-the-alt-right?source=Snapzu.

ranks of today's woke are riddled with gnostic religiosity. Identitarian bands function as "street families" for the
soul.

If fatherlessness and secularization are two aspects of
the decline of the paternal principle, there remains a
third: attachment to country. Here, too, Millennials and
Gen Z stand out. For decades, the decline of American
patriotism among the young has been charted in surveys.
Gallup reports a fifty-year decline in Americans' trust
in both political and nonpolitical institutions (the mili-
tary, the police, organized religion, the media). A headline in *The Hill* in 2019 summarized the point: "Poll:
Patriotism, Religion, Kids, Lower Priorities for Younger
Americans".[27]

Plainly, weakened bonds in one social realm are not
isolated phenomena; one attenuation seems to lead to
another. Filial piety appears to be like a muscle: it strength-
ens when exercised and atrophies when not in use.

Loss of patriotism, loss of faith, and loss of family each
seem to encourage breakdown in the other parts of the
triad. In his groundbreaking 1999 book, *Faith of the Fatherless: The Psychology of Atheism*, sociologist Paul Vitz analyzed one way in which the father-Father connection
might operate.[28] He examined the biographies of prominent atheists across four centuries and argued that each had
experienced some form of "defective fatherhood", such
as absence or abuse. Anger at fathers, Vitz theorized, was
translated into anger at God.

[27] Rebecca Klar, "Poll: Patriotism, Religion, Kids, Lower Priorities for
Younger Americans", *The Hill*, August 25, 2019, https://thehill.com/homenews
/news/458752-patriotism-religion-kids-lower-priorities-for-younger-americans
-poll/.

[28] Paul Vitz, *Faith of the Fatherless: The Psychology of Atheism* (San Francisco,
CA: Ignatius Press, 2013).

In 2013, my book *How the West Really Lost God* connected godlessness with the experiential reality of fatherlessness in another way, to argue that secularization amounted to fallout from disrupted family trees. Together, these works suggest an avenue for future research: Does lacking an earthly father make it harder to believe in a supernatural Father? And might the reverse also be true?

Meanwhile, to understand better how these simultaneous weakenings of filial attachment play out in society, consider two imaginary representative characters: William, born in 1950, and his grandson Brandon, born in 2000.

A member of the Baby Boom generation, William grew up in an intact home. His parents took him and his siblings to church. Two adults in the home meant twice as many warm bodies for driving and organizing. This meant that William, like his siblings, belonged to Boy Scouts, Little League, high school sports, the church youth group, marching band, and other activities.

Though William wasn't much of a flag-waver, he wasn't a flag-burner, either. This was true, in part, because almost every male authority figure William knew had served in World War II or the Korean conflict, and, of course, some of his contemporaries served in Vietnam. "The Star-Spangled Banner" was played without incident before every football and basketball game at his high school.

William married young and had a family. He and his wife found an evangelical church to their liking. He didn't always attend with her, but he did volunteer in the church's soup kitchen. It made him feel good. William also coached Little League, volunteered with the local ambulance corps, and played regular poker games. William smoked cigarettes, especially with friends on his work breaks. His favorite TV show, which he watched with his family, was *Star Trek*. He thought it would be cool if his children or grandchildren ended up traveling in outer space.

William's grandson Brandon, a Zoomer, was born in 2000. His mother—William's daughter—married Brandon's father. The pair split up when Brandon was three. Brandon has no siblings. He rarely saw his father, or his father's side of the family, after the divorce. Given what he has heard from his mother, he doesn't much want to. He thinks of his father, who eventually remarried, as a two-time loser. At age twenty, Brandon has already decided that he won't let any woman entrap him in a marriage. Thanks to the internet, he has other outlets for sex, anyway.

Having a single mom put certain activities off the table. Brandon never joined Little League or the Scouts or other youth groups. He played soccer for his school and loved it. But logistics placed other possibilities, such as travel-team sports, beyond reach. Since he graduated high school, most of Brandon's IRL activity—like much of his activity, period—has been solitary.

Brandon's mom swore off religion at the time of her divorce, so he's rarely been inside a church. When his mom's boyfriend moved in, Brandon started spending most of his time in his room or out of the house. He doesn't pay much attention to politics, but he does watch lots of sports. He likes Colin Kaepernick's FU attitude. Brandon smokes pot by himself. His favorite video game, which he plays alone or with others online, is *Bulletstorm: Full Clip Edition*.

Like other young adults, Brandon spends a lot of time on the internet. During high school, two of his favorite sites were Reddit and 4chan. For a while, Brandon was drawn to the alt-right; he liked that they had an FU attitude, too. As of summer 2020, though, he's been following Signal with growing interest. He likes to keep up with the protests, riots, and street fights with the cops that are being organized using that app. He might move to Portland someday for the politics, or maybe to Colorado for the pot. Brandon thinks it would be cool to skateboard with a real gun.

As these imaginary lives convey, a generational divide has opened between the Boomers and the Millennials and Zoomers. It is a wealth gap over social capital. And it is enormous.

In retrospect, William's attachments to entities other than himself, and larger than himself, were not neutral coordinates of human geography. They informed and enriched his life, not least because they put other people in it—people from whom he could learn, with whom he could connect and network, and through whom he could learn commitments and make common cause.

Brandon's more peripatetic social bonds make his existence very different from his grandfather's. His days are lonelier. His enthusiasms are less tempered by familial and communal influences, hence more volatile. The deficit lies not merely in Brandon's fatherlessness. It is arithmetical, beginning with the subtraction of his father's entire side of the family, which effectively halves the number of Brandon's relatives. The diminution of kin continues with the shrinking number of family members on his mother's side.

As a result, there are fewer people in Brandon's life from whom he might learn essential skills such as negotiation, diligence, compromise, teamwork, delayed gratification, and self-control. If, and when, the time comes for Brandon to become a father, he will have less to impart about all these forms of discipline as well. In sum, Brandon is a poster boy for the trends mapped in Robert D. Putnam's *Bowling Alone: The Collapse and Revival of American Community*—a book that appeared in the very year that this prototypical Zoomer was born.[29]

Of course, there are other variables that diminish Brandon's chances in life. Millennials and Zoomers face economic problems the Boomers did not, especially staggering college debt and the continuing effect on capital of the financial crash of 2008. But dollars and cents may not be the only reason for the wealth-and-opportunity divide. Perhaps the relative economic success of the Boomers is not a matter of business cycles alone. Perhaps the skills and flexibility honed through respecting and negotiating with different kinds of authority are valuable training for a productive life. Perhaps having more siblings rather than fewer, more social ties rather than more screens, and more contemporaries, from whom "social learning" becomes possible, are lifetime pluses.

This much we do know. The streets of Portland—and Kenosha and Baltimore and Rochester, and all the other cities that served in 2020 as proscenia for mob explosions—are full of Brandons. And in a curious coda at a time when race seems to be everywhere, note that it does not matter whether William and Brandon are black, white, or other. The demographic trends that shape their stories and the resulting social wealth gap remain the same.

This brings us to the point that has been missed so far, not only during the long summer of 2020, but throughout

---

[29] Robert D. Putnam, *Bowling Alone: The Collapse and Revival of American Community* (New York, NY: Simon and Schuster, 2000).

the many recent discussions of American disarray, or American unraveling, or just plain *what the hell is happening to America?*

What is happening to America is an excruciatingly painful truth that life without father, Father, and filial piety toward country are not the socially neutral options that contemporary liberalism holds them to be. The sinkhole into which all three have collapsed is now a public hazard. The tripartite crisis of paternity is depriving many young people—especially young men—of reasons to live as rational and productive citizens. As the Catholic theologian Deborah Savage put it recently, reflecting on America's youth: "They have been left alone in a cosmos with nothing to guide them, not even a firm grasp of what constitutes their basic humanity, and no means of finding the way home."[30]

To be sure, all manner of accelerants have made matters worse: the internet, social media, racial prejudice, lax political leadership, scandals within the churches, the coarsening of political conversation, the polarization of the media into clashing armies. So has the metastasizing of the Civil Rights Act, as Christopher Caldwell has observed.[31] A feverishly partisan intellectual class has stoked the flames with critical race theory, charges of "fascism" in America, and other debased characterizations. What Jeane J. Kirkpatrick called "blaming America first" has become the standard classroom narrative for practically every humanities major under the age of seventy.[32]

---

[30] Deborah Savage, "The Return of the Madman: Nietzsche, Nihilism, and the Death of God, circa 2020", *Catholic World Report*, August 10, 2020, https://www.catholicworldreport.com/2020/08/10/the-return-of-the-madman-nietzsche-nihilism-and-the-death-of-god-circa-2020/.

[31] Christopher Caldwell, *The Age of Entitlement: America Since the Sixties* (New York, NY: Simon and Schuster, 2020).

[32] Mary Eberstadt, "The Left Still Blames America First", *Wall Street Journal*, August 19, 2020, https://www.wsj.com/articles/the-left-still-blames-america-first-11597854057.

Doubtless, the collapse of logic on campuses and across media has something to do with declining faith in authority of any kind—and with diminishing patriotism, too.[33]

Even so, the social Rubicon crossed in summer 2020 signals something new. The triply disenfranchised children of the West have achieved critical mass. They have slipped the surly bonds of their atomized childhoods; they have found their fellow raging sufferers and formed online families; and they have burst as a destructive force onto the national consciousness *en masse*, left and right, as never before.

Like Edmund in *King Lear*, who despised his half-brother Edgar, these disinherited young are beyond furious. Like Edmund, too, they resent and envy their fellows born to an ordered paternity, those with secure attachments to family and faith and country.

That last point is critical. Primordial, piteous bitterness is why the triply dispossessed tear down statues not only of Confederates, but of Founding Fathers and town fathers and city fathers and anything that resembles a father, period. It is the reason for generational vituperation toward the Baby Boomers, like the diss of "Okay, Boomer" and the epithet "Karen". It is why bands of what might be called "chosen protest families" disrupt actual family meals. It is why BLM disrupts bedroom communities late at night, where real, live, nonchosen families are otherwise at peace.

Resentment of the Edgars of the world is also the unbidden method beneath the seeming madness of BLM

---

[33] Surveying the past decade of polling research, Karly Bowman of the American Enterprise Institute summarizes, "The few long-term trends that we see on these broader questions from pollsters like Gallup and Pew generally show that young people are less likely than their elders to profess patriotism." Karlyn Bowman and Stephanie Dodd, "Young Love of Country", *American Purpose*, November 30, 2020, https://www.americanpurpose.com /articles/young-love-of-country/; see also Mary Eberstadt, "Why Is There a Patriotism Gap?", *Newsweek*, September 29, 2020, https://maryeberstadt.com /why-is-there-a-patriotism-gap/.

protesters surrounding a home in suburban Portland and demanding that the American flag be taken down, as happened in September 2020.[34] That they were resisted by a neighbor who was black, and a veteran, did not matter. The men and women who think they have no country cannot abide those who have a country, any more than the illegitimate son in *King Lear* can endure his half-brother's enjoying a patrimony.

The dispossessed former children who roamed the streets in search of destruction in 2020 may not be large in number compared to the rest of the United States. And to understand them is not to exonerate them—far from it. But they will not become functioning citizens until the crisis that has unhinged them, and severed them from their own, is ameliorated. In one of the most chilling passages in Shakespeare, Edmund calls on the gods to stand up for bastards. As the United States continues to navigate familial and communal deprivation, Americans will find out whether they do.

[34] Nellie Bowles, "Some Protests against Police Brutality Take a More Confrontational Approach", *New York Times*, September 21, 2020, https://www.nytimes.com/2020/09/21/us/black-lives-matter-protests-tactics.html.

PART IV

WHAT IS THE REVOLUTION
DOING TO THE CHURCH?

8

The Doomed Experiment
of Christianity Lite

Once in a while comes a historical event so packed with unexpected force that it acts like a large wave under still water—propelling us momentarily up from the surface of the times, onto a crest where the wider movements of history may be glimpsed more clearly than before. Such a moment was Benedict XVI's landmark 2009 decision to offer members of the Anglican Communion a fast track into the Catholic Church.[1]

Although commentators quickly dubbed this unexpected overture a "gambit", what it truly exhibited were the characteristics of a move known in chess as a "brilliancy": an unforeseen bold stroke that transforms the game. In the short run, knowledgeable people agreed, this brilliancy might not seem to amount to much; the number of Anglican clergy ushered in this way amounts to drops in the bucket of a universal church.[2]

---

[1] Philip Pullella, "Pope Makes It Easier for Anglicans to Convert", *Reuters*, October 20, 2009, https://www.reuters.com/article/uk-vatican-anglicans/pope-makes-it-easier-for-anglicans-to-convert-idUKTRE59J1UV20091020.

[2] These include former Anglican prelate and Bishop of Rochester Michael Nazir-Ali, who in the course of explaining his decision ended with his "earnest prayer that all those of Anglican heritage will recover the faith brought to England by St. Augustine of Canterbury and his fellow missionaries, as

In the longer run, though, this overture looks consequential in another way. It suggests that the end in sight is not only that of the Anglican Communion, but of something even more consequential: the historical phenomenon of Christianity Lite itself.

By this is meant the multifaceted institutional experiment, beginning but not ending with the Anglican Communion, of attempting to preserve Christianity while simultaneously jettisoning certain of its traditional teachings—specifically, those regarding sexual morality. Surveying the record to date of what has happened to the churches dedicated to this long-running modern religious experiment, a fateful question now appears: Have the exercises in this dissent from traditional teaching contained the seeds of their own destruction, all along? The evidence, preliminary but abundant, suggests that the answer is yes.

If so, then the implications for the future of Christianity are profound. If it is Christianity Lite, rather than Christianity undiluted, that is fatally flawed and unable to sustain itself, then a rewriting of received wisdom, religious and secular alike, is in order. It means that the reasons for the decline in churchgoing may be fundamentally misunderstood. It means that the most unwanted and unfashionable traditional teachings of Christianity demand of the modern mind a new and respectful look. As a strategic matter, it also means that whether orthodoxy or heterodoxy prevails in the intra-Christian struggle may be a matter of religious life or death. Those on the heterodox side tread the same path that the churches of Christianity Lite have followed: down, down, down into religious oblivion.

---

well as the faith of those northern and western saints who evangelized the British Isles as a whole", Michael Nazir-Ali, "From Anglican to Catholic", *First Things*, April 2022, https://www.firstthings.com/article/2022/04/from-anglican-to-catholic.

This use of the phrase *Christianity Lite* is not intended to describe contemporary Protestantism *tout court*—far from it. Plenty of non-Catholic churches—including some of the most vibrant—have not rejected the traditional Christian moral code. Nor is the phrase intended to imply that sexual issues are the *only* theological issues dividing Christendom these days. All kinds of differences remain perennial lightning rods: papal infallibility, the theological status of Mary, the role and ordination of women, predestination, justification, and the rest of the theological controversies historically responsible for tearing Christendom apart.

But standing once again atop that wave in time, one can see clearly that these are *not* the issues that divide the churches of Christianity undiluted from the churches of Christianity Lite today. The latter now define themselves almost exclusively via dissent from traditional teaching about sex.

Certainly ordinary parishioners grasp the point. Ask any contemporary mainline Protestant what most distinguishes his version of Christianity from that of Roman Catholicism, and he will likely deliver some version of this response: *Catholics are still hung up on sex, and we are not. They prohibit things like divorce and birth control and abortion and homosexuality, and we do not.* Moreover, this rendition of the facts would be essentially correct. At this particular moment in Christian history, it is sex—not Mary, or the saints, or predestination, or Purgatory, or papal infallibility, or good works—that divides Christianity into two camps.

How did sex, of all subjects, come to dictate the future shape of the faith? In a sense, the potential was always there. From the earliest adherents onward, the stern stuff of the Christian moral code has been cause for commentary—to say nothing of complaint. "Not all men can receive this saying", the disciples are told when Jesus puts divorce off-limits. Observers throughout history, Christian or not, have agreed. From pagan Rome two thousand years ago to secular Western Europe today, the Church's rules about sex have amounted to saying *no, no, and no* to things about which non-Christians have said *yes* or *why not*.

Even so, to say that modern liberationism has made Christianity Lite inevitable is to fall into a historicist trap. Capital-H history is not in the driver's seat of the human drama; individual people are. Throwing up one's hands at the imperious ways of the *Zeitgeist* also scants a relevant historical point. It was the Anglicans who first started picking apart the tapestry of Christian sexual morality, and quite self-consciously, at that—hundreds of years ago, long before the sexual revolution, and over one particular thread: divorce. In fact, in a fascinating development now visible in retrospect, the Anglican departure over divorce appears as the template for subsequent exercises in Christianity Lite.

For about two centuries, and despite its having been midwifed into existence by the divorcing Henry VIII, the Church of England held fast to the same principle of the indissolubility of marriage on which the rest of Christian tradition insisted. According to a history of divorce called *Untying the Knot*, by Roderick Phillips, "no bishop, archbishop, or incumbent of high Anglican office in the first half of the seventeenth century supported the legalization of divorce."[3]

This early dedication to principle would turn out not to hold, ultimately eroding one priest and one parish at a time. In the United States, Phillips reports, Anglican churches soon were relaxing the strictest restrictions, making divorce more or less easy to come by depending

[3] Roderick Phillips, *Untying the Knot: A Short History of Divorce* (Cambridge, England: University of Cambridge Press, 1991), 33.

upon where one lived. Meanwhile, although the Church of England lagged behind the Episcopalians, by the mid-eighteenth century, divorce was theoretically and practically available by an act of Parliament—a recourse that, although not widely exercised, went to show that with enough clout, exceptions to the principle of indissolubility could be made.

Then came another turn of the theological wheel that could not have been foreseen by the first reformers. As of the General Synod in 2002, divorced Anglicans could now remarry in the church. A spokesman noted carefully at the time: "This does not automatically guarantee the right of divorced people to remarry in Church."[4] But such cautions amounted to powerless incantation. If royals and their consorts could marry in the church—having already married and been divorced from other people—why should every other Anglican not enjoy the same loophole?

Thus does the Anglican attempt to lighten up the Christian moral code over the specific issue of divorce exhibit a pattern that appears over and over in the history of the experiment of Christianity Lite: first, limited exceptions are made to a rule; next, those exceptions are no longer limited and become the unremarkable norm; finally, that new norm is itself sanctified as theologically approved.

The same pattern emerges in another example of the historical attempt to disentangle a thread of moral teaching out of the whole: the dissent about artificial contraception. Here, too, Anglicans took the historical lead. Throughout most of its history, all of Christianity—even divided Christianity—upheld the teaching that artificial

---

[4] "Anglican Church Doors Open for Divorcees to Remarry", *Sydney Morning Herald*, November 16, 2002, https://www.smh.com.au/world/anglican-church-doors-open-for-divorcees-to-remarry-20021116-gdftrb.html.

contraception was wrong.[5] Not until the Lambeth Conference of 1930 was that unity shattered by the subsequently famous Resolution 15, in which the Anglicans called for exceptions to the rule in certain difficult, carefully delineated marital (and only marital) circumstances.[6]

Exactly as had happened with divorce, the Anglicans' okaying contraception was born largely of compassion for human frailty and was dedicated to the idea that such cases would be mere exceptions to the theological rule. Thus, for all that Resolution 15 amounted to a radical break with two millennia of Christian teaching, it also took care to emphasize the limited character of its reform, including "strong condemnation of the use of any methods of conception control from motives of selfishness, luxury, or mere convenience".

Yet just as had happened with divorce, the effort to hold the line at such scrupulously drawn borders soon proved futile. In short order, not only was birth control theologically approved in certain difficult circumstances, but, soon thereafter, it was regarded as the norm. Nor was that all. In a third turn of the reformist wheel that no one attending Lambeth in 1930 could have seen coming, artificial contraception went on to be sanctioned by some prominent members of the Anglican Communion not only as an option, but as the *better* moral choice. By the time of Episcopal Bishop James Pike, only a quarter century or so later, it was possible for a leading Christian to declare (as

[5] See John T. Noonan, *Contraception: A History of Its Treatment by the Catholic Theologians and Canonists*, enlarged ed. (Cambridge, MA: Belknap Press, 1966). He summarizes on p. 6, "No Catholic theologian has ever taught, 'Contraception is a good.'"

[6] As of the passage of Resolution 15 at the 1930 Lambeth Conference, "the bishops of the church whose theology was closest to that of the Roman Catholic Church no longer adhered to an absolute prohibition on contraception." Ibid., 409.

he did) that parents who should not be having a child were not only permitted to use contraception but were, in fact, under a moral obligation to use the most effective forms of contraception obtainable.[7]

Bishop Pike was one of many leaders of Christianity Lite to participate in this same theological process leading from normalization to sanctification. Although the Eastern Orthodox churches sided generally with Rome on the issue of contraception, most Protestants ended up following the same script as the Anglicans—moving one by one from reluctant acceptance in special circumstances, to acceptance in most or all circumstances, and finally, in some cases, to complete theological inversion. No less an authority than the Baptist evangelist Billy Graham, for example, eventually embraced birth control to cope with what he called the "terrifying and tragic problem" of overpopulation.[8]

In just a few decades, in other words—following the same pattern as divorce—contraception in the churches of Christianity Lite went from being an unfortunate option, to an unremarkable option, to the theologically *preferable* option in some instances.

Now consider a third example of the same historical pattern holding in another area: dissent from traditional Christian teachings against homosexuality. As many on both sides of the divide have had occasion to remark, homosexual behavior has been proscribed throughout history by Judaism as well as Christianity, until very, very recently—including in the churches of Christianity Lite. (Henry VIII, to name one prominent example, invoked

---

[7] "Religion: The Birth-Control Debate", *Time*, December 21, 1959, https://content.time.com/time/subscriber/article/0,33009,865161,00.html.

[8] Allan C. Carlson, *Godly Seed: American Evangelicals Confront Birth Control, 1873–1973* (Oxfordshire, England: Routledge, 2011), 125–26.

the alleged homosexuality of the monks as part of his justification for appropriating the monasteries.)

Yet "extraordinarily enough," as William Murchison
puts it in his book *Mortal Follies: Episcopalians and the Crisis
of Mainline Christianity*, "a question barely at the bound-
ary of general consciousness thirty years ago has assumed
central importance to the present life and future of the
Episcopal Church."[9] Why this transformation? In part,
because the reformers at Lambeth and elsewhere did not
foresee something else that in retrospect appears obvious:
the movement from the occasional acceptance of contraception to the celebration of homosexuality would prove
logically sound.

Robert Runcie, for example, former archbishop of
Canterbury, explained his own decision to ordain candidates engaged in homosexual behavior on exactly those
grounds. In a BBC radio interview in 1996, he cited the
Lambeth Conference of 1930 as he observed: "Once
the church accepted artificial contraception they signaled
that sexual activity was for human delight and a blessing even if it was divorced from any idea of procreation.
Once you've said that sexual activity was ... pleasing to
God in itself then what about people who are engaged in
same-sex expression and who are incapable of heterosex-
ual expression?"[10]

Archbishop of Canterbury Rowan Williams has also ret-
rospectively connected the dots between approving pur-
posely sterile sex for heterosexuals on the one hand, and
extending the same theological courtesy to homosexual

---

[9] William Murchison, *Mortal Follies: Episcopalians and the Crisis of Mainline
Christianity* (New York, NY: Encounter Books, 2009), 152.

[10] Quoted in Sharmila Devi, "Ex-Archbishop of Canterbury Ordains
Gays", *UPI*, May 16, 1996, https://www.upi.com/Archives/1996/05/16/Ex
-archbishop-of-Canterbury-ordains-gays/6350832219200/.

acts on the other. As he noted in a lecture in 1989, three years before he became bishop:

> In a church which accepts the legitimacy of contraception, the absolute condemnation of same-sex relations of intimacy must rely either on an abstract fundamentalist deployment of a number of very ambiguous texts, or on a problematic and non-scriptural theory about natural complementarity, applied narrowly and crudely to physical differentiation without regard to psychological structures.[11]

Thus, in retrospect, does the modern Anglican path appear not only unsurprising, but logically (if not exactly religiously) elegant. The rejection of the ban on birth control was not incidental to the Anglicans' subsequent civil disunion over homosexuality and later, transgenderism. It was what started Christianity's sexual civil war.

Moreover, at least as of the December 2009 ordination in Los Angeles of the Episcopal Church's second noncelibate, homosexually active bishop, it is clear that homosexuality's theological status—like that of contraception before it—has moved from an option to a religiously approved option. It therefore joins divorce and contraception in the signature religious cycle of Christianity Lite, conferring on a once prohibited practice a heterodox seal of approval.

Another pattern has also emerged in retrospect from the ongoing experiment in Christianity Lite: rewriting the rules about sex does not, historically speaking, end with sex. Time and again, that rewriting has catalyzed departures from traditional teaching in other areas too.

Consider aforementioned Episcopal bishop James Pike, whose religious evolution illustrates the point. As noted,

---

[11] Quoted in Alexander Lucie-Smith, "What Is Sex for?", *Catholic Herald*, March 23, 2012, https://catholicherald.co.uk/what-is-sex-for/#!.

his views on contraception followed the classic path of Christianity Lite. First, he approved of the use of artificial birth control, then came to insist on it, and finally became chairman of the clergymen's national advisory committee of the Planned Parenthood Federation.[12]

Yet Pike's dissent from traditional Christian teaching, far from being confined to matters of sexual morality, went on to widen over the years. By the 1960s, this pioneer of sexual ethics had also come to question other longstanding Christian beliefs—the Virgin Birth, the Incarnation, the Trinity, and original sin among them. In 1966, Bishop Pike was even formally censured by the Episcopal House of Bishops—a rare rebuke that signifies just how theologically radical he had become, even by the elastic and forgiving standards of the Episcopal Church of America.[13]

There is also the example of the professor Joseph Fletcher, another ordained Episcopal priest who helped to construct Christianity Lite. Thirty-six years stand between the Lambeth Conference of 1930 and the publication of his landmark book, *Situation Ethics: The New Morality*. Primarily concerned (of course) with matters sexual, Fletcher argued that there is "nothing intrinsically good or evil per se in any sexual act" and that, on such grounds, conventional morality deserved jettisoning.[14]

The example of Fletcher shows once more how dissent from core teaching migrates into other doctrinal areas. By the end of his life, this Episcopal priest had parted company

[12] "A Pastor's Take on Birth Control in 1955", *Newsweek* Archives, January 26, 2017 (reprint of a column from January 31, 1955, discussing Bishop Pike and the religious case for birth control), https://www.newsweek.com /religious-leader-case-birth-control-1955-548678.

[13] Edward H. Pitts, "Pike Demands a Trial", *Christianity Today*, October 11, 1966, https://www.christianitytoday.com/ct/1966/october-11/pike-demands -trial.html.

[14] Murchison, *Mortal Follies*, 161.

with Christian orthodoxy on one hot-button issue after another: abortion, infanticide, cloning, euthanasia, and more. Coming full circle, he would later identify himself as an atheist.

Bishop John Shelby Spong of Newark, N.J., was another prominent Episcopalian who began his career by spurning the usual unwanted rules, and went on to spurn much more. *Time* magazine called his *Living in Sin: A Bishop Rethinks Human Sexuality* (1988) "probably the most radical pronouncement on sex ever issued by a bishop".[15] It advocated the by-now familiar list of sexual selections from the contemporary cafeteria menu—from blessing homosexual unions to all the rest of "freeing the Bible from literalistic imprisonment".

Yet Bishop Spong's radicalism, though jumpstarted by sex, did not end there, any more than Bishop Pike's or Reverend Fletcher's did. It, too, broadened to include dissent from Christian doctrine. Spong said he believed in God but was not a theist, for example, and he also denied that Jesus either performed miracles or rose from the dead. So consistent is his record that R. Albert Mohler Jr., the traditionalist president of the Southern Baptist Theological Seminary, once remarked of Spong that "heretics are rarely excommunicated these days. Instead, they go on book tours."[16]

These examples affirm an institutional point: even in the hands of its ablest defenders, Christianity Lite has proven to be incapable of rewriting rules about sex alone. Once

---

[15] *Time*, quoted on the back cover of John Shelby Spong, *Living in Sin: A Bishop Rethinks Human Sexuality* (New York, NY: HarperCollins, reprint edition, 1988).

[16] R. Albert Mohler Jr., "Heresy in the Cathedral", *Albert Mohler* (blog), August 16, 2007, https://albertmohler.com/2007/08/16/heresy-in-the-cathedral-2.

bedrock teaching is dispensed with, the temptation appar- ently becomes overwhelming to put other inconvenient doctrines on the chopping block. To switch metaphors, which came first, the egg of dissent over sex or the chicken of dissent over other doctrinal issues? Christianity Lite can- not seem to have one without the other.

This same pattern of dissent over sexuality, followed by decline in both church membership and practice, also appears clearly in the other churches of the Protestant main line. The speed with which Protestant practice and principle collapsed together bear scrutiny, particularly in a moment when some Catholics seem eager to follow the same doomed playbook.

In 1930, for example, the initial reaction among Amer- ica's Lutherans to Lambeth's Resolution 15 was disbelief bordering on hostility. Margaret Sanger was denounced in an official Lutheran newspaper as a "she devil", and numerous pastors took to the pulpits and op-ed pages with blistering complaints about the Anglicans' theological capitulation.[17] Nonetheless, by 1954, the Lutherans, too, were encouraging contraception in order to make sure that any child born would be valued "both for itself and in relation to the time of its birth".[18] By 1991, the Evangeli- cal Lutheran Church was not only affirming contraception as good, but also officially urging widespread instruction in "sex education" and pregnancy prevention for youngsters.

In all, it has been an about-face that would have shocked the Lutherans of yesteryear—beginning with Martin Luther himself, who once called contraception "far more

[17] Robert Baker, "Medicating against Motherhood?", *Hausvater Project*, May 2010, https://www.hausvater.org/articles/214-medicating-against-motherhood .html.

[18] Marcia Clemmitt, "Birth-Control Debate: Should Americans Have Easier Access to Contraception?", *CQ Researcher*, 15, no. 24 (June 24, 2005).

atrocious than incest or adultery". None of which is to say that the motivation behind these changes is elusive; to the contrary, it could not be more transparent. As biblical scholar Carl R. Trueman has observed, "Christian elites [today] try to persuade the secular world that they aren't so bad—no longer in terms of Enlightenment conceptions of reason, but in terms of the disordered moral preoccupations of the day."[19]

Also like the Anglicans, the Evangelical Lutheran Church in America (ELCA) has proven that one thread could not be teased out of the tapestry without others coming undone too. In 1991, its *Social Statement on Abortion* found that abortion could be a morally responsible choice in certain circumstances.[20] That same year, the Churchwide Assembly (CWA), the leading legislative body of the church, affirmed that "gay and lesbian people ... are welcome to participate fully in the life of the congregations of the Evangelical Lutheran Church."[21] Less than two decades later, in 2009, official tolerance for individuals had transposed into something else: official approval of the practice of homosexuality, enshrined in the decision to ordain noncelibates.

Thus the ELCA, the largest and most liberal of the Lutheran bodies of America, has suffered the next consequence arising from the experiment of Christianity Lite:

---

[19] Carl R. Trueman, "The Failure of Evangelical Elites", *First Things*, November 2021, https://www.firstthings.com/article/2021/11/the-failure-of -evangelical-elites.

[20] Evangelical Lutheran Church in America, *A Social Statement on Abortion*, adopted by the Churchwide Assembly, August 28–September 4, 1991, https:// download.elca.org/ELCA%20Resource%20Repository/AbortionSS.pdf.

[21] Evangelical Lutheran Church in America, "Welcoming Gay and Lesbian People", Social Policy Resolution CA 95.06.50, adopted by the 1995 Churchwide Assembly, http://download.elca.org/ELCA%20Resource%20Repository /Welcoming_LGBT_PeopleSPR95.pdf.

the institutional implosion of the churches that have tried it. The body faces the same fate as the Anglican Communion: threats of schism, departing parishes, diminishing funds, and the rest of the institutional woes that have gone hand in hand with the abandonment of dogma.

The fate of the Episcopal Church and the ELCA also threatens the rest of the mainline Protestant churches—the Presbyterian Church (USA), the United Church of Christ, the United Methodist Church, and the American Baptist Church. As Joseph Bottum has observed, "The death of the Mainline is the central historical fact of our time: the event that distinguishes the past several decades from every other period in American history."[22] Across the board, donations are down, attendance is down, attendance of the young is down especially, and missionaries—a relevant proxy for vibrancy of belief—are diminishing apace. Even the kind of social work for which Christian churches have been renowned is also down. Mainline Protestant volunteerism, according to the Barna Group, dropped a shocking 21 percent between 1998 and 2008 alone.[23]

While decline and disarray have so ruthlessly visited the mainline churches of American Protestantism, more traditional-minded Protestant institutions have proved comparatively robust. At least since sociologist Dean Kelley's work in the 1970s, culminating in the book *Why Strict Churches Are Growing*, observers have tried to make sense

[22] Joseph Bottum, "The Death of Protestant America: A Political Theory of the Protestant Mainline", *First Things*, August 2008, https://www.firstthings.com/article/2008/08/the-death-of-protestant-america. For his analysis of the animadversions of Protestant spirituality following the death of the mainline churches, see *An Anxious Age: The Post-Protestant Ethic and the Spirit of America* (New York, NY: Image Books, 2014).

[23] "Report Examines the State of Mainline Protestant Churches", *Barna*, December 7, 2009, https://www.barna.com/research/report-examines-the-state-of-mainline-protestant-churches/.

of that phenomenon.[24] Abortion—about which some traditional-minded Protestant churches are more absolutist now than they used to be—is one example. Even more unexpected is the rethinking by some prominent Protestants of artificial contraception.[25]

This reconsideration is one of the least familiar and potentially consequential religious developments in the United States. It is happening because new leaders are taking to heart the lessons of experience, and trying to avoid the withering visited on the Anglican Communion and other mainline Protestant churches.

Does the relaxing of dogma drive people from church? Or does the decline in attendance push leaders to relax dogma? As with the previous discussion of dissent, one does not need to grasp the answer in all its causal complexity. The trajectory is plain enough. As the legendary convert and teacher Monsignor Ronald Knox observed some eighty years ago, "The evacuation of the pew and the jettisoning of cargo from the pulpit" have been going on side by side for as long as Christianity Lite has been attempted.[26] As with doctrinal dissent, it seems, where one appears, the other is sure to follow.

In sum, Christianity Lite has left enough evidence in its wake for us to judge that colossal experiment a failure. The effort to throw out the unwanted bathwater of the sexual code takes the proverbial baby—the rest of Christian practice and belief—along with it. What accounts for this

---

[24] Dean Kelley, *Why Strict Churches Are Growing: A Study in Sociology of Religion* (New York, NY: Harper & Row, 1962).

[25] See Mary Eberstadt, *How the West Really Lost God: A New Theory of Secularization* (West Conshohocken, PA: Templeton Press, 2013), chap. 10, for more citations.

[26] Ronald A. Knox, *The Beliefs of Catholics* (San Francisco, CA: Ignatius Press, 2000), chap. 1, "The Modern Distaste for Religion".

epochal, perhaps even counterintuitive outcome—one that surely would have shocked the architects of this pivotal religious turn, who longed only for Christianity with a happier human face?

One answer seems self-evident. If enough people over enough time shrug at the injunction to be fruitful and multiply, eventually their churches will become barren too. Studies clinch the point. In research published in 2005 in *Christian Century*, three sociologists (Andrew Greeley, Michael Hout, and Melissa Wilde) argued that "simple demographics" between 1900 and 1975 explained around three-quarters of the decline in mainline churches (Episcopal, Lutheran, Presbyterian, and Methodist).[27] By contrast, they pointed out, during those same years membership rose in more conservative Protestant churches (Baptist, Assembly of God, Pentecostal, and so on). The difference was that women in the former churches began using artificial contraception before women in the latter ones—in sum, "The so-called decline of the Mainline may ultimately be attributable to its earlier approval of contraception."

A second reason for the self-destruction of Christianity may be this rule of thumb: people who reject demanding rules also come to chafe at easier ones. In the 1950s, almost half the population of the Church of England attended services on Sunday.[28] By 2000, that figure was around 7 percent, and that includes Charismatic and Pentecostal affiliates. Such plummets are now common across the churches of Christianity Lite. Clearly, making life easier for people in the pews has not made them likelier to sit there.

[27] Michael Hout, Andrew Greeley, and Melissa J. Wilde, "The Demographic Imperative in Religious Change in the United States", *American Journal of Sociology* 107, no. 2 (2001): 468–500.

[28] Steve Bruce, "Christianity in Britain, R.I.P.", *Sociology of Religion* 62, no. 2 (2001): 191–203.

The observation that Christianity Lite spells historical doom is not defeatist, but neither is it triumphalist. Christian orthodoxy may never enjoy what the world understands by victory, or even a social turnaround from the current Western status quo. Many Catholics, including voices of influence within the Church, still wish to jettison the same unwanted baggage as their Protestant brethren. This is all the more reason to emphasize the point that churches which chose this route are dying.

No doubt centuries will be required before yesterday's houses of worship become whatever they will ultimately become—shelters, mosques, nightclubs, concert halls, nursing homes. Meanwhile, other questions about the future shape of Christianity remain to be answered. What will become of tradition-minded Protestants elsewhere on the planet, beginning with the Global South, who oppose Christianity Lite? From the top of any historical wave, one can only spy so much.

Still, it is no trivial thing to glimpse on the horizon the beginning of the end not only of Anglicanism as the world has known it, but also of the other churches that joined their fates to that of Christianity Lite. It is hard to overstate how momentous their unraveling is—or how bracing a slap in the modern face. After all, if there is a single point to which enlightened people have been agreeing for a long time now, it is that certain antiquated notions must go for the sake of a kinder, gentler Christianity.

It would be more than passing strange if those very anachronisms turned out to be pieces that could not be sacrificed after all—not without having the rest of the house fall down, anyway. Then again, it would not be the first time in Christian history that a slab rejected by some of the builders turned out to be a cornerstone.

9

What Causes Secularization?

On the surface, the title of this chapter amounts to a simple query. It is only three words long. It seems as if the towering apparatuses of modern sociology, with metrics and spread-sheets, and innumerable data spun in innumerable ways, ought to be able to answer the question handily.

Yet, at the same time, "What causes secularization?" is also a subversive question, because it turns the conceptual tables on the long-running Western conversation about Christianity upside down. Ever since the Enlightenment, religious belief has been treated like the outlier, the weird thing, the artifact from the past that needs "explaining". "What causes secularization?" disputes that framing. It makes the point that today's secularism, not organized religion, is the anomaly whose origins deserve scrutiny.

The point is fair. Recorded history affirms that human beings, generally speaking, are theotropic. People across cultures and across time lean toward God or gods; mankind divided by languages is nevertheless united by *some* notion of transcendence, *some* belief in a realm beyond the senses. At times it seems as if the supernatural is banished from the living room, only to reenter through the back door. New Age practices and beliefs, and new forms of "spiritualism", for example, continue to fill some of the vacuum left by the decline of organized American Christianity. As a writer for the *New Yorker* put it, describing the similarities between and the impetus for today's spiritualism and yesterday's Spiritualism,

> today's Spiritualists have something in common with their Victorian predecessors, situated as they are in another era of rapid technological change and increasing secularization; the Internet and virtual reality are the present moment's photography and telegraphy, technologies so advanced that they approach the uncanny; then as now, a vast penumbra of proto-spiritualists surround the true believers. No longer persuaded by orthodox religious accounts but also not satisfied with pure materialism, they experiment with psychics, crystals, tarot, and astrological charts, or simply swap stories of the eerie and the unexplained.[1]

The point is that people do not leave their spiritual home for *nothing*, but rather for some other kind of faith, even if by another name. During the era of the "burned-over district" in upstate New York in the early nineteenth century, for example, several new sects sprung up that drew converts away from the Congregationalist, Baptist, Methodist, and other Protestant churches of the time.[2] Some of these startups would later become global, such as the Church of Jesus Christ of Latter-Day Saints and the Seventh Day Adventists—continuing to pull new members of the faithful away from their preexisting religious practices, in the same way that Christianity's tremendous

[1] Casey Cep, "Why Did So Many Victorians Try to Speak with the Dead?", *The New Yorker*, May 24, 2021, https://www.newyorker.com/magazine/2021/05/31/why-did-so-many-victorians-try-to-speak-with-the-dead.

[2] For a history, see Whitney R. Cross, *The Burned-Over District: The Social and Intellectual History of Enthusiastic Religion in Western New York, 1800–1850* (Ithaca, NY: Cornell University Press, 1982).

growth in Africa during the last few decades has drawn believers such as Cardinal Robert Sarah away from animism, and other Africans away from Islam, syncretism, and related indigenous faiths that preceded today's Christian proselytizing.[3]

Such examples suggest that the widely accepted post-Enlightenment dichotomy between faith and no faith is simplistic, even misleading; more likely, everyone believes *something*—including the fabled "nones", as discussed ahead. It may be that "secularization" itself is a blanket term that obscures more than it clarifies about where religious belief really "goes". For our purposes here, though, "secularization" can continue as useful shorthand as we ponder this other way of phrasing the opening question on secularization: How is it that societies once markedly Christian have become less so? This is surely one of the most interesting puzzles in history—the more so because its outlines are starker with each passing decade.

Consider some examples from the United States. The fabled "nones", mainly young people who check "none of the above" when asked to describe their religious faith, are fabled for a reason: their growth has been dramatic. In 2021, according to Pew Research, the percentage of "nones" was 6 percent higher than it had been five years before, and 10 percent higher than in 2011.[4] Conversely, self-described Christians made up 63 percent of the same

[3] For an account of Christianity's stunning growth in Asia and Africa during the end of the twentieth century into the twenty-first, see John Micklethwait and Adrian Wooldridge, *God Is Back: How the Global Revival of Faith Is Changing the World* (London: Penguin, 2010), 16 especially.

[4] Gregory A. Smith, "About Three-in-Ten U.S. Adults Are Now Religiously Unaffiliated", *Pew Research Center*, December 14, 2021, https://www.pew research.org/religion/2021/12/14/about-three-in-ten-u-s-adults-are-now -religiously-unaffiliated/.

population in 2021, down from 75 percent a decade earlier. Young America is increasingly unchurched.

Similar patterns can be found across the other societies of the West once profoundly influenced by the Christian faith. In Australia, "nones" were 6.7 percent of the population in 1971; in 2021, they amounted to 38.9 percent.[5] While Christianity remained the "most common" religion, weighing in at 43.9 percent, it has steadily declined apace, losing over one million adherents between 2016 and 2021. In Italy, where over 70 percent of the population still identifies itself as "Catholic", the number of citizens attending church at least once a week dropped to twelve million in 2020, down six million from 2010.[6] Also in keeping with other Western nations, as the same report noted, "the most prayerful were the citizens aged over 75 years, whereas the lowest number of individuals attending religious services at least once a week was recorded in the age group between 18 and 24 years." In England and Wales, the "Christian" affiliation is hovering at 51 percent for the first time in recorded history.[7]

Even far more observant Poland is not immune to these same trends. Poland's Statistical Institute of the Catholic Church, for example, reports that weekly attendance at Mass was 53 percent in 1987. By 2011 it had dropped to less than 40 percent. It continues to decline steadily. According to the Polish bishops' conference, in 2020 only

[5] "Religious Affiliation in Australia", Australian Bureau of Statistics, April 7, 2022, https://www.abs.gov.au/articles/religious-affiliation-australia.

[6] "Number of People Who Attend Religious Services at Least Once a Week in Italy from 2006–2020," Statista, June 21, 2022, https://www.statista.com/statistics/576085/weekly-church-attendance-in-italy/.

[7] Kaya Burgess, "Losing Our Religion: Christians Poised to Become a Minority", *Sunday Times*, December 18, 2021, https://www.thetimes.co.uk/article/losing-our-religion-christians-poised-to-become-a-minority-5mzf6dw99.

36.9 percent of the country's Catholics attended Sunday Mass, down almost two percentage points from 2018.[8]

On it goes across the Continent and into Canada, New Zealand, Australia, and the rest of the West.[9] Statistics aside, there are also other measures of Christianity's recession from the public square to consider, from the commercial success of the new atheism during the late 1990s, to the changing legal norms about religious expression, to the manifest growth in public animosity towards the Catholic Church in particular—especially after the *Dobbs* decision reversing *Roe v. Wade*.[10]

What happened here? As Charles Taylor has put the question rhetorically, Why was belief in God unremarkable five hundred years ago, whereas now it is considered in need of explanation?[11]

Begin by understanding what has *not* happened. Many people have supposed, to name one example of a going theory, that prosperity drives out God. In the minds of sophisticated secularists, religion is Marx' famous "opiate of the masses"—a consolation prize for the poor and backward. If this conventional account of secularization

---

[8] "Catholic Church in Poland Records 1.3% Fall in Sunday Mass Attendance in 2019", *Catholic News Agency*, December 11, 2020, https://www.catholic newsagency.com/news/46879/catholic-church-in-poland-records-13-fall-in -sunday-mass-attendance-in-2019. These data were compiled by the Institute for Catholic Church Statistics.

[9] For a detailed discussion of secularization in individual countries, see Mary Eberstadt, *How the West Really Lost God: A New Theory of Secularization* (West Conshohocken, PA: Templeton Press, 2013), especially footnotes to the introduction and chap. 1.

[10] See, for example, Richard W. Garnett, "Anti-Catholic Attacks after *Dobbs*", *First Things*, June 29, 2022, https://www.firstthings.com/web-exclusives/2022 /06/anti-catholic-attacks-after-dobbs, and Joe Bukuras, "Vandalism of Churches, Pro-Life Pregnancy Centers Continues after Dobbs", *Catholic News Agency*, July 5, 2022, https://www.catholicnewsagency.com/news/251725 /vandalism-of-churches-pro-life-pregnancy-centers-continues-after-dobbs.

[11] Charles Taylor, *A Secular Age* (Cambridge, MA: Belknap Press, 2007), 32.

were sound—if it correctly predicted who was religious, and why—then one would reasonably expect that the poorer and less educated people are, the *more* religious they would be.

But the fact is that these stereotypes are *not* correct. One can find too many cases in which the opposite is true.[12]

Consider British historian Hugh McLoed's research on religiosity in London between the 1870s and 1914. In a book called *Class and Religion in the Late Victorian City*, he documents that among Anglicans in London during that period, "the number of ... worshippers rises at first gradually and then steeply with each step up the social ladder".[13] Put differently, "the poorest districts thus tended to have the lowest rates of [church] attendance, [and] those with large upper-middle-class and upper-class populations the highest."[14] Religious reality in the example of Victorian London ran contrary to stereotype. "Only a small proportion of working-class adults", he observes, "attended the main Sunday church services" (Irish Catholics being the sole exception).[15]

British historian Callum G. Brown makes the same point about religiosity in England during those years: contrary to common wisdom, "the working class were irreligious, and ... the middle classes were the churchgoing bastions of civil morality."[16]

Much the same pattern can be found in the United States today. It suggests that material well-being does not

[12] For an expanded consideration of the relationship between social class and churchgoing, see Eberstadt, *How the West*, chaps. 2, 3, and 4.

[13] Hugh McLeod, *Class and Religion in the Late Victorian City* (Hamden, CT: Archon Books, 1974), 28–29.

[14] Ibid., 29.

[15] Ibid.

[16] Callum G. Brown, *The Death of Christian Britain: Understanding Secularization, 1800–2000* (London: Routledge, 2001), 149.

explain declining religious belief. One of the most thorough examinations of American religiosity was published in 2010 by sociologists Robert D. Putnam and David E. Campbell. Their data in *American Grace: How Religion Divides and Unites Us*, confirm that elevated social status does not correlate with irreligiosity—quite the opposite. During the first half of the twentieth century, the authors observe, college-educated people participated in church life more than did those with less education. After the 1960s, overall decline began to accelerate, but attendance tended to be higher among the educated than among the less educated. The authors conclude, "This trend is clearly contrary to any idea that religion is nowadays providing solace to the disinherited and dispossessed, or that higher education subverts religion."[17]

The point of this statistical excursion is not to invent a neo-Calvinist stereotype connecting success in life to divine favor. It is rather to observe that intuition alone is an unreliable guide to charting the course of secularization—and this fact calls conventional accounts of religious decline into question. Prosperity and education do not exile God.

Consider another theory. Is secularization the consequence of the twentieth century's two world wars, as others have suggested? Did Western men and women lose their faith in a benevolent Creator when faced with the unprecedented horrors and body counts of World War II—the invasions, the bombing of civilians, the Holocaust?

To visit Auschwitz is to understand why some might think so. It is indeed hard to stare into a pit full of human ashes so large that it still exists almost eight decades later,

---

[17] Robert D. Putnam and David E. Campbell, *American Grace: How Religion Divides and Unites Us* (New York, NY: Simon and Schuster, 2010), 253.

without grasping a little of the problem of theodicy. And yet the idea that God died in Auschwitz or in some other of the twentieth century's horrors is also problematic.

First, it is hard to see how countries with different experiences of those wars—neutral Switzerland, vanquished Germany, victorious Great Britain—can be more or less equally irreligious today. The war trauma theory also does not explain why countries uninvolved in the wars should exhibit the same trends. Philip Jenkins, most notably, has tracked the falloff in religious practice in Latin America, noting "signs of secularization ... that would have been unthinkable not long ago".[18] In addition to the data on attendance and belief, the liberalization of abortion laws in countries that were once Catholic strongholds is an impressive case in point. Moreover, it is hard to square the same theory with the religiosity that persisted in parts of the East under Soviet domination despite severe oppression: monasteries expropriated, clergy persecuted, church properties seized, and the rest. Most notably, Poland, home to many of the worst ravages of World War II, was and remains more faithful than its Western counterparts

But the most convincing evidence against the war theory is historical. The end of World War II was, in fact, followed by a religious boom—one that occurred not only in the United States, but across the West. Those years were such that Will Herberg, the most prominent sociologist of religion in America, could observe in his classic book *Protestant-Catholic-Jew* that the village atheist was a figure of

---

[18] Philip Jenkins, "A Secular Latin America?", *Christian Century*, March 12, 2013, https://www.christiancentury.org/article/2013-02/secular-latin-america. See also his book, *Fertility and Faith: The Demographic Revolution and the Transformation of World Religions* (Waco, TX: Baylor University Press, 2020), which affirms the argument of this chapter: family formation and religious formation are joined at the root.

the past and that even agnosticism seemed to be waning.[19] That is how resurgently observant America in the 1950s had become.

This same religious boom was also pan-Western in scope. It applied to the vanquished as well as the victorious, the neutral as well as everyone else, the economically devastated as well as the prosperous. In the public realm, the rhetoric of leaders was pro-Christian in a way that today strikes us as unbelievable. German Chancellor Konrad Adenauer, to take just one example, said in a famous speech in Cologne that Germany had gone over to the Nazis because its Christianity hadn't been strong enough.[20] Christianity's vibrancy in those years is affirmed by its commercial clout; witness the extraordinary popularity of Christian themes in mid-century Hollywood blockbusters. In sum, the religious boom of the immediate postwar era in and of itself refutes two ideas: one, that Christian decline is inevitable; and two, that the world wars in and of themselves caused secularization.

Sociology can map trends with data, but about the elemental question of why people stop going to church—or for that matter, why they start—the going theories come up short. Rather, and crucially, religion waxes and wanes in the world—strong one moment, weaker the next.

This brings us to an explanatory variable for secularization that demands far more attention than it has received in the sociology of religion. That variable is the family— more specifically, the relationship between the health of the family and the health of Christianity. To study the

---

[19] Will Herberg, *Protestant-Catholic-Jew: An Essay in American Religious Sociology* (Chicago, IL: University of Chicago Press, 1983), 46–47.

[20] Hans-Peter Schwarz, *Konrad Adenauer: A German Politician and Statesman in a Period of War, Revolution and Reconstruction: From the German Empire to the Federal Republic, 1876–1952* (Oxford, NY: Berghahn Books, 1995), 357.

historical timeline is to see that religious vibrancy and family vibrancy go hand in hand. Conversely, so do religious decline and family decline: where one is found, expect the other.

Return to those years of postwar religiosity as a test case. The religious boom overlay perfectly with a much more familiar phenomenon: the Baby Boom—which in turn was preceded by a boom in marriage. Across the West, the Second World War was followed by an increase in marriage and babies. The Baby Boom and the religious boom did not just *happen* to go hand in hand. Plainly, each augmented the other. Plainly, something about living in families increases the likelihood that people will go to church and believe in God.

In fact, there is more than one such "something". First, family life encourages religious life because mothers and fathers will seek out a like-minded moral community in which to situate their children. Childrearing is hard work, and the enormity of the undertaking weighs heavily on most parents. No wonder so many seek a community to help them with it.[21] In this prosaic way, the creation of a family literally drives some people to church.

Conversely, as has not been so well studied but is obviously also true, the lack of a family removes a social incentive for church. Depending on what has disrupted familial bonds, fractured families might also interfere with religious formation in other ways. Recall Paul Vitz' work on atheism, connecting the dots between rejection of an earthly father and rejection of an unearthly Father. The generalized anger and loss felt by many children of divorce might easily spill over into other realms, including anger

---

[21] A Baptist minister and radio host once told me that almost every new person who enters his congregation is a mom or dad with a baby in arms.

at *Whoever* invented such a broken world in the first place. Popular music of the 1990s and 2000s affirms the connection; rage at the world and rage at the fractured family were two of its dominant themes.[22]

There is another way in which becoming a mother or father appears to affect religiosity. The very experience of birth—of simply becoming and *being* mothers and fathers—transports many people into a religious frame of mind. The primal bond between parent and child is for many the most powerful in the human drama.

Social science affirms that religiosity exerts a protective power over marriage and family life; religious married people are considerably less likely to divorce, and religious people are more likely to marry in the event of a nonmarital pregnancy.[23] Conversely, the experience of marital breakup appears to affect religious affiliation negatively; women who divorce in middle age, for example, are significantly less likely to be religiously involved later in middle age.[24] Simultaneously, religious faith operates as a preventive force on family breakup; according to a 2018 study at Harvard University's Institute for Quantitative Social Science, religious practice reduces divorce by as much as 50 percent.[25] Data from the General Social

[22] Mary Eberstadt, "Eminem Is Right", *Policy Review*, December 2004/January 2005, https://www.hoover.org/research/eminem-right.

[23] W. Bradford Wilcox, "Religion and the Domestication of Men", *Contexts* 5, no. 4 (Fall 2006): 42–46, https://journals.sagepub.com/doi/pdf/10.1525/ctx.2006.5.4.42.

[24] Kimiko Tanaka, "The Effect of Divorce Experience on Religious Involvement: Implications for Later Health Lifestyle", *Journal of Divorce and Remarriage* 51, no. 1 (2010): 1–15.

[25] Shanshan Li, Laura D. Kubzansky, and Tyler J. VanderWeele, "Religious Service Attendance, Divorce, and Remarriage among U.S. Nurses in Mid and Late Life", *Plos One*, December 3, 2018, https://journals.plos.org/plosone/article?id=10.1371%2Fjournal.pone.0207778.

Survey confirm that Christians, in particular, are more likely to marry, and less likely to divorce, if they are regular churchgoers.[26]

These linkages point to another way of understanding religious decline: the West is secularizing, in part, because so many are no longer marrying, because divorce has become a common fact of life, and because many are failing to have children. The correlations between religiosity and family formation cannot be dismissed as mere coincidences. Consider an example from the converse end: Scandinavia. Who pioneered the postwar unmarried Western family and its close ally, the welfare state (whose arguably critical role in secularization is also part of this picture)? Scandinavia. What is arguably the most atomized place in the Western world today, as measured by, say, the number of people who do not live in a family at all? Scandinavia again. According to *Eurostat*, just over half of Swedish households are now singletons. In Finland, that percentage is over forty.[27]

Plainly, these phenomena are related. Family is a driver of religious faith, not just vice versa. Scandinavia is just one example of the "double helix" of family and faith at work. What has happened in the Scandinavian family—shrinkage and fracture—has transformed the Scandinavian churches. The causal relationship is two-way. Each institution needs the other to reproduce.

Understanding the symbiosis between family and faith makes the "puzzle" of secularization less of a puzzle. It

---

[26] Brian Hollar, "Regular Church Attenders Marry More and Divorce Less Than Their Less Devout Peers", *Institute for Family Studies*, March 4, 2020, https://ifstudies.org/blog/regular-church-attenders-marry-more-and-divorce-less-than-their-less-devout-peers.

[27] "Over Half of Sweden's Households Made Up of One Person", *Eurostat*, May 9, 2017, https://ec.europa.eu/eurostat/web/products-eurostat-news/-/ddn-20170905-1.

also casts doubt on the notion that the falloff in religious observance amounts to mankind coming to its collective senses about the nonexistent Deity, and moving on. That caricature may capture what secular people believe. But it is not what the historical record suggests about the relationship between participating in small-*c* human creation and believing in Creation.

Another fact about kinship is also germane. Christianity as a religion is itself intrinsically familial—meaning that it both privileges the family and tells its own story via intensely domestic metaphors, time and again. This is a faith that begins, after all, with a baby and a Holy Family—a mother who suborns herself to the child completely and a loving, adoptive father. The story of the Incarnation makes no sense outside this familial frame. Likewise, Jesus' dying act is one of reasserting the primacy of family; he tells the apostle John to be a son to Mary, and he tells Mary to be a mother to John.

How could a story like that *not* cause confusion in a postrevolutionary time like our own, when so many either repudiate primordial family bonds or lack them in the first place? How can one even explain God the benevolent Father to a teenager who has never known such a figure? Such is one example of how postrevolutionary mores hinder religious education. These impediments to faith shape the practice of going to church—or not. The fact of shared custody of children, where many children spend alternating weekends with split-up parents, is one example. Switching between different households every Saturday or Sunday *by itself* makes consistent religious instruction and practice not only inconvenient, but practically impossible.

Secularization also continues to gain ground because of unacknowledged but powerful competition from the rival secularist faith analyzed in chapter 3. For example, when polled in 2021 about why they were leaving Catholicism, 64 percent of Italian respondents said that they disagreed with the Church's position on "social issues".[28] Which "issues" are most likely objects of dispute? Feeding the hungry? Caring for the poor or the sick? Here, as elsewhere, the real reason people are leaving the Church is their desire for sexual expression unimpeded by religious authority.

In sum, the changes in family formation that are now common across the Western world make the Christian religious story seem more incoherent, remote, or unwanted— or all three—in a society habituated to postrevolutionary behavior. Evangelization in such a time demands creativity of a new order. It is analogous to explaining to someone who has only lived in apartment buildings what it might be like to live in a house—especially when he has never seen a house. The effort is not impossible. But it explains some of what must be overcome if Christianity is to compete effectively against the secularist church, do-it-yourself spiritualism, New Ageism, and the rest, let alone traditional competitors like other organized religions.

To summarize: The decline of Christianity in the West is not incidental to the change in Western family patterns. These epic phenomena are twinned and cannot be understood apart from one another.

Just as insufficient academic attention has been paid to the role of family collapse, so is there little discussion about the social fallout of secularization. Why does it matter whether Christianity diminishes? It matters, in part, because social justice matters—and because the Church by its very nature cannot abandon the quest for the common good.

---

[28] "Number of People Who Attend Religious Services at Least Once a Week in Italy from 2006 to 2020", Statista, August 23, 2021, https://www .statista.com/statistics/576085/weekly-church-attendance-in-italy/.

As noted in chapter 2, given the opportunity to choose between humanitarianism on the one hand, and dogmatic purity concerning the sexual revolution on the other, activists choose the revolution. The National Abortion Rights Action League (NARAL) and like-minded groups have sued pregnancy centers across the country—that is, charitable institutions where desperate women can receive free sonograms and aid and support for having a baby, as well as help with items ranging from medical care to baby furniture and other everyday needs.[29] Pro-abortion groups have repeatedly sought to impede these pregnancy centers via burdensome ordinances and by other political means. Following the *Dobbs* case reversing *Roe v. Wade* in 2022, opposition to the centers intensified. Senator Elizabeth Warren, for example, expressed her hope of shutting down every last one in Massachusetts.[30]

In conjunction with the attorney general of California, for example, NARAL sponsored legislation requiring the state's crisis pregnancy centers to counsel pregnant women about abortion and contraception—in other words, forcing Christians into speech that violates their consciences, with the callous intention of driving religious believers out of the business of helping desperate women. The United States Supreme Court in 2018 reversed a lower court decision upholding the law, largely on grounds that it impeded free speech. The case was revelatory in another way: it exposed the bare-knuckle tactics common among

[29] See Mark Sherman, "Supreme Court Voids Part of Crisis Pregnancy Center Law", *PBS News Hour*, June 26, 2018, https://www.pbs.org/newshour/nation/supreme-court-voids-part-of-crisis-pregnancy-center-law.

[30] Christopher Bell, "Elizabeth Warren Smears Pro-Life Charities", *Wall Street Journal*, July 5, 2022, https://www.wsj.com/articles/elizabeth-warren-smears-pro-life-charities-mothers-maternity-homes-children-baby-pregnancy-center-11657053639.

activists for whom choosing an abortion overrules all else, including the comfort and safety of pregnant women who choose not to abort.[31]

The United States is not the only example of the two-way street between secularist desires to "own" Christians, and secular indifference to the consequences. Suing charitable institutions that fail to conform to un-Christian or anti-Christian demands spills across borders. In Belgium, a Catholic nursing home that refused to allow one of its patients to be killed on site was fined 6,000 euros by the government on the grounds that "the nursing home had no right to refuse euthanasia on the basis of conscientious objection."[32] In Canada, "medical assistance in dying", or MAID, became legal in 2016, and in 2021 was amended to expand access to assisted dying, including to people whose natural end was not imminent.[33] The legal besieging of Christian adoption agencies for failing to recant what the Bible says about family is also international in scope; the last remaining Catholic adoption operation in Great Britain, for example, was shuttered in 2012 following years of legal battles.[34]

Believers who feel their Christianity to be a burden in these postrevolutionary times might recall the marginalized

[31] Victoria Colliver, "Supreme Court Sides with Crisis Pregnancy Centers in Fight over California Law", *Politico*, June 26, 2018, https://www.politico.com/story/2018/06/26/supreme-court-crisis-pregnancy-centers-673183.

[32] Simon Caldwell, "Catholic Care Home in Belgium Fined for Refusing Euthanasia", *Catholic Herald*, July 4, 2016, https://catholicherald.co.uk/catholic-care-home-in-belgium-fined-for-refusing-euthanasia/.

[33] "Get the Facts: Canada's Medical Assistance in Dying (MAID) Law", *Dying with Dignity Canada*, https://www.dyingwithdignity.ca/end-of-life-support/get-the-facts-on-maid/.

[34] "Ruling Forces Last Catholic Adoption Agency in England and Wales to Cease Adoptions", *Catholic News Agency*, August 20, 2010, https://www.catholicnewsagency.com/news/20619/ruling-forces-last-catholic-adoption-agency-in-england-and-wales-to-cease-adoptions.

and castoff people who depend on the churches—and who depend on Christians *being* Christians. As noted in chapter 2, on "the new intolerance", secularism's tolerance for collateral human damage is unacceptably high. This truth, manifest in today's burgeoning religious-liberty skirmishes, will only become more patent over time. As it does, believers will better understand the moral downside of the antagonistic church of secularism. Meanwhile, the path to religious restoration runs as it always has: through the hearth.

10

The Prophetic Power of
Humanae Vitae

Just as shortchanging of the poor and weak lends credit to
the alternative of Christianity, so do logic and empiricism
continue to vindicate the same ancient teachings rejected
by the postrevolutionary order. This evolving side of the
empirical ledger, too, might make a dent on people of
the present and future.

In 2008, on the fortieth anniversary of one of the most
famous and reviled documents in modern history, *First
Things* published an essay of mine called "The Vindication of *Humanae Vitae*". Citing contemporary evidence
from many sources, including sociology, psychology,
history, and contemporary women's literature, the piece
argued:

> Four decades later, not only have the document's signa-
> ture predictions been ratified in empirical force, but they
> have been ratified as few predictions ever are: in ways its
> authors could not possibly have foreseen, including by
> information that did not exist when the document was
> written, by scholars and others with no interest what-
> ever in its teaching, and indeed even inadvertently, and

in more ways than one, by many proud public adversaries of the Church.[1]

Of course, to say that proof abounds is not to say that a valid argument falls on happy ears—not fifty years ago, not ten years ago, and not today. The promise of sex on demand, unencumbered by constraint, is a collective temptation second to none. That is why, since the invention of the birth control pill, resistance to the traditional Christian code has been unremittingly ferocious, and why so many in the laity and clergy wish that this rule—among others—were less taxing. Even so, today, as before, to confuse "hard" with "wrong" is a fundamental error. Leaning into *reality*, there is only one conclusion to be drawn from the empirical evidence. It is the same conclusion that was visible ten years ago and that will remain visible ten or one hundred or two hundred years from now: the most unwanted encyclical in modern times is also the most prophetic and explanatory.

Set aside theology, philosophy, ideology, and other abstractions, and enumerate the latest realities vindicating *Humanae Vitae*, one by one.

The first empirical reality was visited in detail in chapter 1, "More Paradoxes of the Sexual Revolution": increased use of contraception has also increased abortion. There is also the fact that contraception and abortion are bound together juridically. Michael Pakaluk has outlined the legal logic:

> As regards jurisprudence, the fruit of contraception is abortion. Until the 1960s, Comstock Act laws were on the books in many states, making the sale of contraceptives

[1] Mary Eberstadt, "The Vindication of *Humanae Vitae*", *First Things*, August 2008, https://www.firstthings.com/article/2008/08/002-the-vindication-of -ihumanae-vitaei.

illegal even to married couples. These laws were over-
turned in 1965 by the Supreme Court's muddled *Gris-
wold* decision. But by 1973—only eight years later—the
Supreme Court in *Roe v. Wade* had inferred from the right
to contraception a right to abortion.[2]

Legal reasoning about the freedom to contracept became
the precondition of the freedom to abort. Or, one might
say, freedom to contracept was never enough. Given that
every method of birth control has a failure rate, only the
backup of abortion could make contraception as reliable as
people hoped it would be.

History connects the same causal dots. The push to lib-
eralize abortion laws in countries around the world did
not begin until the first third of the twentieth century, as
birth control devices came into wider circulation. American states did not start liberalizing abortion laws until after
the federal approval of the birth control pill in 1960. *Roe
v. Wade* comes after the Pill, not before. As a matter of
historical fact, the mass use of contraception called forth
the demand for more abortion.

In part because fifty years of experience have established
reality number one, a second reality has become evident.
People outside the Catholic Church—most notably,
though not only, some leading Protestants—have come
to see *Humanae Vitae* in a new and more favorable light.

As noted in chapter 8, more and more Protestant voices
now question yesterday's nonchalance about the wisdom of adapting to the times, hoping to spare their own
churches the fate visited on those that have embraced it.
This reconsideration is far from a majority view—yet. But
it manifests what any minority view must have in order to

[2] Michael Pakaluk, "The Link Between Contraception and Abortion",
First Things, January 23, 2018, https://www.firstthings.com/web-exclusives
/2018/01/the-link-between-contraception-and-abortion.

win over others: evidence and moral energy. Consider a few examples.

"Many evangelicals are joining the discussion about birth control and its meaning. Evangelicals arrived late to the issue of abortion, and we have arrived late to the issue of birth control, but we are here now."[3]

> —R. Albert Mohler Jr., president, Southern
> Baptist Theological Seminary, 2010

"For evangelicals, an anticontraception position is not seen as exclusively Roman Catholic, as it would have been in the past."[4]

> —Jenell Paris, anthropologist, Messiah College, 2012

"More Protestants Oppose Birth Control."[5]

> —New York Times headline, 2012

"Whenever current events touch on life issues, evangelicals like me become increasingly uncomfortable with the contraception culture. We realize we have much more in common with Catholics, who revere life, than the radical feminists who revere the rights of women above all else."[6]

> —Julie Roys, evangelical author and blogger, 2012

---

[3] R. Albert Mohler Jr., "The Pill Turns 50—TIME Considers the Contraceptive Revolution", *Albert Mohler* (blog), April 26, 2010, https://albert mohler.com/2010/04/26/the-pill-turns-50-time-considers-the-contraceptive -revolution.

[4] Quoted in Mark Oppenheimer, "Many Evangelicals See Something to Admire in Candidates' Broods", *New York Times*, January 20, 2012, https:// www.nytimes.com/2012/01/21/us/more-protestants-oppose-birth-control .html.

[5] Ibid.

[6] Julie Roys, "Christians and the Contraception Culture", *Roys Report* (blog), March 1, 2012, https://julieroys.com/rethinking-contraception/.

"Protestants have done themselves a disservice by ignoring *Humanae Vitae*'s substantial statement on human anthropology and sexuality.... Protestants would be well-served to study Paul VI's encyclical and take heed of its warnings."[7]

—Evan Lenow, professor at Southwestern
Baptist Theological Seminary, 2018

As noted in chapter 8, these second thoughts among Protestants and other non-Catholics are less a radical break from Christian tradition than a return to it.

Back in 1930 at the pivotal Lambeth Conference, Charles Gore, the bishop of Oxford, objected to Resolution 15. He had "manifold reason to believe that in the case of Birth Prevention the 'very strong tradition in the Catholic Church' has been in the right, and has divine sanction".[8] The move by some Protestants toward *Humanae Vitae* today is in part a tacit declaration that, in retrospect, the bishop of Oxford's side might have been the right one.

In Africa, both Protestants and Catholics lean toward traditionalism. Here as elsewhere in history, the maxim delivered by sociologist Laurence R. Iannaccone holds: "Strict churches are strong"—and concomitantly, lax churches are weak.[9] It is in the tradition-minded subcontinent that Christianity has grown explosively in the years since *Humanae Vitae*—as opposed to those nations whose Christian leaders have struggled, and struggle still, to change the rulebook.

---

[7] Evan Lenow, "Protestants and Contraception", *First Things*, January 2018, https://www.firstthings.com/article/2018/01/protestants-and-contraception.

[8] Charles Gore, "Lambeth on Contraceptives", *Project Canterbury* (London: Mowbray, 1930), available online at http://anglicanhistory.org/gore/contra1930.html.

[9] Laurence R. Iannaccone, "Why Strict Churches Are Strong", *American Journal of Sociology*, 99, no. 5 (1994).

As the Pew Research Center has reported, "Africans are among the most morally opposed to contraception."[10] Substantial numbers of people in Kenya, Uganda, and other sub-Saharan countries—Catholic and otherwise—agree with the proposition that contraception use is "morally unacceptable"; in Ghana and Nigeria, it is more than half the population. Despite decades of secular proselytizing, many in Africa have resisted the attempts of reformers to bring them into line with the secular Western sexual program—which includes, of course, diminishing the number of Africans.

Nigerian-born Obianuju Ekeocha, author of the book *Target Africa: Ideological Neo-Colonialism of the Twenty-First Century*, wrote an open letter to Melinda Gates, whose foundation dedicates impressive resources to spreading birth control among Africans: "I see this $4.6 billion buying us misery. I see it buying us unfaithful husbands. I see it buying us streets devoid of the innocent chatter of children.... I see it buying us a retirement without the tender loving care of our children."[11]

Africans are not the only intended beneficiaries of campaigns to expand the contraceptive *Weltanschauung*. Nor are they alone in abjuring the idea that the world would be better off with fewer of them in it. As one notable Indian targeted with the same message some years back put it, "It is futile to hope that the use of contraceptives will be restricted to the mere regulation of progeny. There is hope for a decent life only so long as the sexual act

[10] Michael Lipka, "Africans Among the Most Morally Opposed to Contraception", *Pew Research Center*, April 16, 2014, https://www.pewresearch.org/fact-tank/2014/04/16/africans-among-the-most-morally-opposed-to-contraception/.

[11] Obianuju Ekeocha, *Target Africa: Ideological Neo-Colonialism of the Twenty-First Century* (San Francisco, CA: Ignatius Press, 2018).

is definitely related to the conception of precious life."[12] The author of these sentences is not Elizabeth Anscombe, whose famous 1972 essay "Contraception and Chastity" defended *Humanae Vitae* with this same logic.[13] It is instead Mahatma Gandhi—one more non-Catholic to affirm the reasoning behind Christian moral teaching. "I urge the advocates of artificial methods to consider the consequences", he explained elsewhere. "Any large use of the methods is likely to result in the dissolution of the marriage bond and in free love."[14]

Fear that "public authorities" might "impose" these technologies on the citizenry—as *Humanae Vitae* also warned—rightly endures. This happened in China via its barbaric one-child policy, replete with forced abortions and involuntary sterilizations, from 1980 to 2021. A softer kind of coercion has appeared in the United States and other Western nations where efforts have been made to link desired outcomes with mandatory birth control. In the 1990s and beyond, for example, some U.S. judges backed state-imposed implantation of long-term contraceptives in women convicted of crimes.[15] Such implied force has provoked criticism by (among others) the American Civil Liberties Union (ACLU): "The recent attempts

[12] M. K. Gandhi, *Self-Restraint vs. Self-Indulgence* (Ahmedabad, India: Navajivan Publishing House, 1947), 149

[13] G. E. M. Anscombe, "Contraception and Chastity", in Janet E. Smith, ed., *Why Humanae Vitae Was Right: A Reader* (San Francisco, CA: Ignatius Press, 1993), 121–47.

[14] Quoted on the website of Bombay Savodaya Mandal/Gandhi Book Centre, Gandhian Public Charitable Trust, https://www.mkgandhi.org /momgandhi/chap59.htm.

[15] Tamar Lewin, "Implanted Birth Control Device Renews Debate over Forced Contraception", *New York Times*, January 10, 1991, https://www .nytimes.com/1991/01/10/us/implanted-birth-control-device-renews -debate-over-forced-contraception.html.

to coerce women to use Norplant represent a reversion to an era of overt racism and eugenics."[16]

Reality number three concerns the state of modern women. Contraception, it was and is perennially asserted, has made them happier and freer than ever before. Has it? Evidence points to the contrary—from social science suggesting that female happiness across the United States and Europe has been declining over time,[17] to the dolorous notes so often struck in academic and popular feminism, to the growing worry among secular women that marriage has become impossible and it is time to go it alone. More could be added to the ledger suggesting that *Humanae Vitae* was right to spy a widening chasm between the sexes. Consider in passing two snapshots.

In 2012, Amazon U.K. announced that E. L. James' *Fifty Shades of Grey* had replaced J. K. Rowling's Harry Potter books as the best-selling volume in its history.[18] This signals an extraordinary commercial demand *by women* for the tale of a rich and powerful man who humiliates, bullies, and commits violence against a woman, over and over.

Sadomasochism is a prominent theme elsewhere in popular culture—including, again, popular women's culture. Concerning the fashion industry, John Leo observed, "I first noticed the porn-fashion connection in 1975, when *Vogue* magazine ran a seven-photo fashion spread featuring a man in a bathrobe battering a screaming model in

[16] "Norplant: A New Contraceptive with the Potential for Abuse" (undated), ACLU website, https://www.aclu.org/other/norplant-new-contraceptive-potential-abuse.

[17] Betsey Stevenson and Justin Wolfers, "The Paradox of Declining Female Happiness", *National Bureau of Economic Research*, May 2009, https://www.nber.org/papers/w14969.

[18] Reuters Staff, " 'Fifty Shades...' Outsells Potter on Amazon UK", *Reuters*, August 1, 2012, https://www.reuters.com/article/books-fiftyshades-record-id UKL6E8J1LDH20120801.

a lovely pink jumpsuit ($140 from Saks, picture by Ave-don)."[19] *Harper's Bazaar* has seconded the point: "Long before *Fifty Shades* fever hit, designers have been mining BDSM for sartorial inspiration. From literal crops to all forms of waist, wrist, and ankle ties—not to mention the sheer volume of leather—it's clear Christian Grey would be proud."[20]

Implied and overt violence against women saturates video games and, of course, pornography. The sadomaso-chistic look has become widespread in popular music; the number of globally recognized female singers who have *not* paid homage to pornography and sadomasochism is vanishingly small. Does the success of *Fifty Shades* tell us that men have become so hard to get that any means of finding one will do, no matter how degrading?

This brings us to still another reality: fifty years into the sexual revolution, one of the most pressing, and growing, issues for researchers is not overpopulation, but *underpop-ulation*. The essay on *Humanae Vitae* marking the fortieth anniversary maintained that the overpopulation scares of the late 1960s were just that: scares. They happened not-so-coincidentally to be ideologically useful to partisans who wanted the Church to change its moral teaching. The original piece noted:

> So discredited has the overpopulation science become that this year Columbia University historian Matthew Connelly could publish *Fatal Misconception: The Struggle to Control World Population*, and garner a starred review in

[19] John Leo, *Two Steps Ahead of the Thought Police* (London and New York, NY: Routledge, 1994), 223.

[20] Kerry Pieri, "The Best Bondage on the Runway", *Harper's Bazaar*, February 13, 2015, https://www.harpersbazaar.com/fashion/fashion-week/g5263/best-runway-bondage-fashion/.

> *Publishers Weekly*—all in service of what is probably the
> single best demolition of the population arguments that
> some hoped would undermine church teaching. This is
> all the more satisfying a ratification because Connelly is so
> conscientious in establishing his own personal antagonism
> toward the Catholic Church.... *Fatal Misconception* is deci-
> sive [secular] proof that the spectacle of overpopulation,
> which was used to browbeat the Vatican in the name of
> science, was a grotesque error all along.[21]

The past decade has made reality transparent. Not only is
"overpopulation" a shifting ideological chimera, but the
reverse obtains. The newest disease of civilization across the
infertile and graying West is the thoroughly documented
"epidemic" of loneliness.[22]

A further reality to ponder is historical, and worth reiterating at a time when hope burns eternal in some precincts that the Catholic Church will cease its intransigent
insistence on supposedly retrograde points of doctrine. The
churches that have accommodated themselves to the sexual revolution have imploded from within. As a headline
in *The Guardian* put it simply in 2016, on the eve of a con-
tentious conference at Lambeth where African representatives of the Anglican Communion dissented once more
from changing moral teaching: "The Anglican Schism
over Sexuality Marks the End of a Global Church."[23]

In 1930, Christians would have been shocked if told
that the doctrinal war over sex would shatter the Anglican

---

[21] Eberstadt, "Vindication".

[22] See Mary Eberstadt, *Primal Screams: How the Sexual Revolution Created Identity Politics* (West Conshohocken, PA: Templeton Press, 2018), chap. 2, for a
summary of the sociology of loneliness in various Western nations.

[23] Andrew Brown, "The Anglican Schism over Sexuality Marks the End of
a Global Church", *Guardian*, January 8, 2016, https://www.theguardian.com
/commentisfree/2016/jan/08/anglican-schism-sexuality-end-global-church
-conservative-african-leaders-canterbury.

Communion; that parts of the Communion would go to legal war over churches and jurisdictions as well as doctrine; that the separation of North and South, Episcopal and Anglican, Africa and Europe, would yield divisions and subdivisions, sorrow and acrimony, on a global scale.

According to David Goodhew, editor of the 2016 volume *Growth and Decline in the Anglican Communion: 1980 to the Present*, research by Jeremy Bonner on the Episcopal Church shows: "Around 2000 serious decline set in.... Average Sunday attendance dropped by nearly one third between 2000 and 2015.... The rate of baptism has been cut almost in half over a thirty-year period.... The most dramatic data is for marriages.... In 2015 the Episcopal Church married less than a quarter of the number it married in 1980."[24] As Goodhew also noted, "If we believe Christian faith is good news, we should be seeking its proliferation, and be worried when it shrinks." In 2018, revisiting more recent statistics on the Episcopal Church, he summarized, "The rate and relative timing of decline varies markedly, but almost all dioceses are in decline to some degree.... Data on congregation size and congregational closures suggest that the long-term aging of the church continues, as do its deleterious effects."[25]

The facts of religious history make their own case. Disaster descended on the Anglican Communion for doing exactly what dissenters from *Humanae Vitae* want the Catholic Church to do: make exceptions to rules that people dislike. Surely anyone urging Rome to follow Lambeth's lead today must first explain how Catholicism's fate will be different.

[24] David Goodhew, ed., *Growth and Decline in the Anglican Communion: 1980 to the Present* (London: Routledge, 2016).

[25] David Goodhew, "Facing More Episcopal Church Decline", *Covenant*, August 30, 2018, https://covenant.livingchurch.org/2018/08/30/facing-more-episcopal-church-decline/.

A final reality vindicating *Humanae Vitae* has endured all along. The attempt to pick and choose among Church teachings, which became ubiquitous beginning in the 1960s, was self-destructing from the start. Father Paul Mankowski stated the problem brilliantly:

> [T]he religious stance that emerged in the rejection of *Humanae vitae* ... involves the belief that there is a higher, or deeper, or at any rate more reliable mediator of God's will than the teaching Church. This point cannot be stressed too much. If the Church is wrong in *Humanae vitae*, the judgement that it is wrong can only be made with reference to some standard. That standard, obviously, cannot be the Church herself; some contend that it is moral intuition, others a more academically respectable reading of Scripture or of the history of doctrine; still others some comprehensive system of ethics or logic. But the crucial point is that whatever standard is taken as fundamentally reliable, *this standard judges the Church, and is not judged by her.* Here is the real revolution incited by the Pill; next to it the rise in promiscuity is a mere flutter.[26]

"Manuscripts don't burn." In Mikhail Bulgakov's twentieth-century masterpiece *The Master and Margarita*, a despairing author trapped under oppressive Soviet rule tries to destroy his own unpublished book in a fire—only to learn, in the redemptive denouement, that it is impossible. Too dangerous to publish under Communism, *The Master and Margarita* itself would not appear until almost thirty years after the novelist's death in 1940—whereupon it became, and remains, a literary sensation around the world. Bulgakov could see with his soul what he would never

---

[26] Paul V. Mankowski, *Jesuit at Large: Essays and Reviews by Paul V. Mankowski, S.J.*, edited and with an introduction by George Weigel (San Francisco, CA: Ignatius Press, 2021), 52–53 (emphasis added).

witness with his eyes. "Manuscripts don't burn" became an immortal rallying cry on behalf of the indomitable nature of truth. Truth, artistic or otherwise, may be unwanted, inconvenient, resented, mocked in all the best places—even harassed, suppressed, and forced underground. But that does not make it anything other than truth.

In this moment of watchfulness inside and outside the Church, a global fellowship knows the truths of *Humanae Vitae* and related teachings *as* truths, however unwanted or hard. They are among the latest pilgrims in a line stretching two thousand years back. They have sacrificed to stand where they do, and they sacrifice still—including by relinquishing the good opinion of a mocking world.

These cradle Catholics and converts and reverts, fellow-traveling non-Catholics, clergy and laity alike have the consolation of one final *reality*, which may be the most indispensable of all. Whatever the anxieties of the moment, however prominent or widespread the disgruntlement, the evolving record continues to vindicate Paul VI's encyclical. *Humanae Vitae* does not burn.

EPILOGUE

What Are Believers to Do?
The Cross amid the Chaos

This book, like its predecessor, makes the case that Catholic moral teaching is vindicated by sources outside the Church. The fact that more and more Christians and non-Christians alike reject that teaching does not affect its truth value one whit. If the argument holds, a question will naturally have occurred to readers that lies beyond the scope of the case itself: Where does this interpretation leave Christians, who now wonder how to live *as* Christians, at a time when resistance to the Church has become obstreperous and calcified?

An insight by novelist extraordinaire Evelyn Waugh illuminates across the passage of nearly a century. It appeared in a disarmingly casual account that he gave to a newspaper in 1930, about the reasons for his conversion to the Catholic Church. Waugh summarized that decision in twenty-eight neat words. He said, "In the present phase of European history the essential issue is no longer between

This epilogue is adapted from a speech given on September 15, 2021, to the Society of Catholic Social Scientists upon reception of their annual Pius XI Award for Building up a True Social Science. The event was cosponsored by the Catholic University of America's Sociology Department and Institute for Human Ecology.

Catholicism, on one side, and Protestantism, on the other, but between Christianity and Chaos."[1]

Christianity, or Chaos. In a sense, the choice between the two has been perpetual since the Resurrection. But to shrug that it was ever thus, and to throw up one's hands before the world, is a dodge—especially for Catholics, especially now, in a moment when many are tempted for more reasons than one to do just that. Believers are called to read the signs of the times, not to whine about them. Today's Catholics cannot begin to live as Christians without first staring this thing in the face and seeing the distinctive characteristics of Chaos in this moment. What broad shapes appear?

First is that we continue to live in the age spied by Matthew Arnold, Henri de Lubac, Aleksandr Solzhenitsyn, and other religious clairvoyants of the past two centuries: the modern age, whose drama consists of successive waves of secularization, encroaching ever more insistently on territories previously thought to be God's, and God's alone.

The second certainty, equally conspicuous, is that the forms of Chaos characteristic of the first quarter of the twenty-first century are distinct from those that have gone before. Compare this era, for example, with Waugh's own. In 1930, the year he entered the Church, one world war was already behind mankind, even as another impended. In the lifetime of people like him, spanning roughly the first half of the twentieth century, Chaos had a different signature. It resided in war, dislocation, and stupendous carnage.

Despite that carnage, social pillars still stood firm in Europe and America and other heirs to Western civilization. Individual families were ravaged by the wars, but the

---

[1] Donat Gallagher, *The Essays, Articles, and Reviews of Evelyn Waugh* (New York, NY: Little, Brown and Company, 1984), 103.

institution of the family was not. Demonic Nazi anthropology had its day, as Communist anthropology would, too, but outside those malignant precincts, a Christian understanding of creation and redemption and meaning still prevailed across the Anglosphere, Western Europe, the Captive Nations of the East, and elsewhere.

The Catholic Church was steadfast as well. In 1930, Pius XI was pope. He would go on to found Vatican Radio the very next year, "to proclaim the Gospel in the world", as he said with jubilance. Though Chaos was starting to insinuate itself in novel forms into some Protestant churches, the Barque of Peter appeared exempt—as Evelyn Waugh pointed out when he cited the "coherent and consistent" nature of Catholic teaching as the predominant reason for his conversion.

As even that short summary shows, although we are only ninety-some years removed from 1930, it feels more like ninety-some light-years. Consider a quick checklist of the scene today.

First, there is compounding family Chaos, brought on by a radical social experiment now six-plus decades in the making. Elemental human bonds have been frayed and cut, and the institution of the family has been weakened, on a scale never seen before.

Second, and symbiotic, there is also compounding psychic Chaos of all kinds. For decades, the rise in mental illness has been documented beyond dispute. Anxiety, depression, and other afflictions resulting from disconnection and loneliness have become endemic, especially among the youngest and most frail.[2] Irrationalism has come unbound.

---

[2] See, for example, "The State of Mental Health in America", *Mental Health America*, available online at https://www.mhanational.org/issues/state-mental -health-america. Its "2022 Key Findings" include: in 2019, just prior to the

Third, there is political Chaos. Though its causes are many, the dissolution of clan and community leave their marks here too. To put it rhetorically: How could the unattached and dispossessed people of the early twentieth century produce anything *but* a disordered public language?

Fourth, there is anthropological Chaos of a wholly new order. The Western world is gripped by an identity crisis. In its latest form, magical thinking about gender has escaped from the academy and now transforms society and law—magical thinking so preposterous that little children could call it out. In a shocking descent unlike any in recorded history, many people today no longer even know what little children know—namely, who they are. Once more, irrationalism is unbound.

Fifth, there is intellectual Chaos. Outside a few faithful institutions, American education, especially elite education, has been hiding in a postmodern cuckoo's nest for decades. People who do not believe in truth now run institutions charged with discerning it. An atheist has lately been elected chief chaplain at Harvard. Why not? If there is no truth, there are no contradictions. Across the humanities, irrationalism is not only unbound. It rules.

Sixth, and most consequential, there is Chaos of a new order and significance among Catholics across the Western world. It arises from people who want to transform Church teaching—and from their animus against other

COVID-19 pandemic, almost 20 percent of adults experienced a mental illness. "Suicide ideation" among adults has increased every year since 2012. Almost 20 percent of youths aged twelve to seventeen experienced major depression. Rates of substance use were rising before the pandemic. These and related findings about the parlous state of mental health, especially among the young, have been documented in many venues. See, for example, Kim Tingley, "There's a Mental-Health Crisis Among American Children. Why? The Pandemic Is Not the Only Reason", *New York Times*, March 23, 2022, https://www.nytimes.com/2022/03/23/magazine/mental-health-crisis-kids.html.

people who hold to the truth of that teaching. This same animus assumes a pious mien in public, as leaders proudly brandishing the Catholic label just as proudly defy the *Catechism* and soft-pedal or ignore key points of canon law, day in and day out. Magical thinking drives this kind of Chaos too. The label "pro-abortion Catholic" makes as much logical sense as "atheist chaplain" or "former man". All participate in the same signature irrationalism. All demand that Aristotle and his law of noncontradiction be cancelled—that both "A" and "Not-A" must be believed at once.

What can be discerned by staring into this void, which has become the inescapable companion that makes some American Catholics more anxious than ever before? What reveals itself should stiffen our spines. In every case, Chaos has been whipped into catastrophic strength by secularization itself. In the time to come, however long the reckoning, this spells trouble for the legacy of secularism and inadvertently endorses the Church.

The rise in mental distress and the decline of organized religion, for example, are not randomly circulating cosmic pinballs. Social science confirms that people who have robust social bonds are more likely to thrive than people who do not.[3] Religious faith confers those bonds. Social science also shows that the fractured family and other forms of isolation increase the risks of anxiety, depression,

[3] See, for example, the data in "Religion's Relationship to Happiness, Civic Engagement and Health around the World", *Pew Research Center*, January 31, 2019, https://www.pewresearch.org/religion/2019/01/31/religions-relationship-to-happiness-civic-engagement-and-health-around-the-world/, which summarizes: "People who are active in religious congregations tend to be happier and more civically engaged than either religiously unaffiliated adults or inactive members of religious groups, according to a new Pew Research Center analysis of survey data from the United States and more than two dozen other countries."

substance abuse, loneliness, and other vexations. Religious belief and participation lower them.[4] All these stressors have been exacerbated by the Western flight from God. Consider once more that the most unchurched generation in America, the "nones", is also the most mentally afflicted. Again, the loss of the capital-F Father and the contemporary loss of so many earthly fathers dovetail.

Secularization also increases family Chaos. By normalizing divorce, fatherlessness, and abortion, mankind has inflicted wounds on itself whose measure has only begun to be taken. What starts at home does not stay at home. The lost boys and girls of family Chaos now pour into the streets, frantically trying to substitute identity politics for the primordial bonds of which they've been deprived. Identity politics is a pitiful attempt at emotional alchemy by souls desperate for connection. It, too, signals tacit exculpation for the Magisterium's uncompromising teachings.

As for the Chaos besetting the Church, this, too, is rooted in the desire to jettison age-old teachings about sin in exchange for the approval of peers. It has become standard to speak of "conservative" Catholics and "liberal" Catholics. But political labels deceive. The real religious divide is between Catholics who want powerful

---

[4] According to one roundup of the data, for example, of 93 observational studies about the relationship between religiosity and depression, two-thirds found that religious people had lower rates of depressive disorder and fewer symptoms. A review of 7 clinical trials and 69 observational studies on anxiety found that half of them demonstrated that religious people have lower levels of anxiety. In another example, 57 out of 68 studies on suicide reported fewer suicides or more negative attitudes toward suicide among religious people. Finally, in a review of 134 studies about the relationship between religiousness and substance abuse, 90 percent found less substance abuse among the religious. Simon Dein, "Religion, Spirituality, and Mental Health", *Psychiatric Times* 27, no. 1 (January 10, 2010), https://www.psychiatrictimes.com/view/religion-spirituality-and-mental-health.

secular trends to influence and transform the Church, and Catholics who do not. It is between souls who believe the *Catechism* is true, and souls who want to edit it with a red pen supplied by a disapproving secularism. The real divide is between Catholics who want temporal demands to trump the Cross, and Catholics who believe that the Cross cannot be trumped.

The point here is not religious triumphalism. It is that secularization is exacting costs in one realm after another—and secularized tastemakers, inside or outside the Church, do not acknowledge that compounding toll. And so it falls to others, including countercultural scholars, to illuminate that record instead. Such work is vital in this moment for two reasons. First, because today's Chaos causes multiple forms of suffering that might be ameliorated if their true origins are understood. Second, because today's Chaos amounts to unintended proof that Christianity, and the Judaism from which it drank, offers an account of human nature that is more congruent with facts, evidence, and intuition than the stunted, materialist alternative.

There is a truth amid today's confusions that has gone too long unsaid. Our secularizing culture is not just any culture. Our secularizing culture is an inferior culture. It is small of heart. It defines suffering down. It regards the victims of its social experiments not as victims, but as acceptable collateral damage justified in the name of progress.

This is secularism's unspoken secret. It is also secularism's greatest vulnerability.

The mission to define suffering down can be seen, for example, in efforts that would recast the horrors of prostitution as anodyne "sex work". It drives the attempts to normalize pornography, ignoring the calamitous costs to men and women and romance. It powers the push to shut down emergency pregnancy centers and adoption agencies, indifferent to whether babies and children and poor people need them. It whitewashes data about suicide rates, eating disorders, substance abuse, and other indices of mental distress, including among the transgender population.[5] Similarly does secularism overlook other suffering, especially among the children and teenagers of the postrevolution, when acknowledging such harms might jeopardize political agendas.

One more quotation helps to summarize the importance of countering the just-so stories told by Chaos. Historian Christopher Dawson wrote that "the survival of a civilization is dependent on the continuity of its educational tradition."[6] The secularized academy has abdicated its vocation. It repudiates continuity. It makes a mockery of the Western patrimony. In the struggle to hold fast to the Cross amid today's Chaos, countercultural scholars are the first line of defense. This is true not only today, but for those who will read the postrevolutionary record in the decades and centuries ahead.

---

[5] See, for example, Elizabeth W. Diemer et al., "Gender Identity, Sexual Orientation, and Eating-Related Pathology in a National Sample of College Students", *Journal of Adolescent Health* 57, no. 2 (August 2015):144–49, https://www.jahonline.org/article/S1054-139X(15)00087-7/fulltext. In this study, a survey of 300,000 students found that transgender participants were four times as likely to experience eating disorders as other students. See also Varun Warrier et al., "Elevated Rates of Autism, Other Neurodevelopmental and Psychiatric Diagnoses, and Autistic Traits in Transgender and Gender-Diverse Individuals", *Nature Communications* 11, no. 3959 (August 7, 2020), https://www.nature.com/articles/s41467-020-17794-1. This study of 600,000 adults found that transgender and gender-diverse adults were between three and six times more likely to be diagnosed as autistic compared with cisgender adults. It reported further that diagnoses of depression, attention deficit hyperactivity disorder, and obsessive-compulsive disorder were also elevated in transgender and gender-diverse adults compared with other adults.

[6] Christopher Dawson, *The Crisis of Western Education* (Washington, DC: Catholic University of America Press, 2010), 5.

These scholars of tomorrow will look back in astonishment, and perhaps pity, at today's magical thinking. They will need facts, figures, arguments, and evidence about the human costs of today's experiment in secularization.

Someday, a re-evangelized civilization might contemplate the beginning of the twenty-first century and try to take the measure of its Chaos. Those people of the future will understand that the counterculture spoke truth into the void of this time and gave voice to the voiceless in a day of defiance. As the legacy of the rebellion against creation seems finally to be summoning scrutiny outside the Catholic Church, that more enlightened civilization may turn out to be closer than anyone has yet guessed.

ACKNOWLEDGMENTS

Thanks first to Cardinal George Pell for his gracious fore-word. It is a privilege to know of his encouragement and to benefit from his immense wisdom.

Chapter 1, "More Paradoxes of the Sexual Revolution" was first delivered as a speech at Hillsdale College in 2018 and then adapted for publication at *The Catholic Thing*. The epilogue, first delivered as a speech to the Society of Catholic Social Scientists, was also published by *The Catholic Thing*. I am grateful to Robert Royal, TCT editor and head of the Faith and Reason Institute, for his enduring support, and to Hannah Russo for her assistance.

Chapters that have been adapted with permission from essays in the journal *First Things* include "The New Intolerance", "From Revolution to Dogma: The Zealous Faith of Secularism", "Men Are at War with God", "The Fury of the Fatherless", and "The Prophetic Power of *Humanae Vitae*". Thanks to two more abiding friends, former editor Joseph Bottum and current editor R. R. Reno, for their encouragement.

The original version of "Two Nations, Revisited", chapter 5, appeared first in the summer 2018 issue of *National Affairs*; thanks to editor Yuval Levin and the team for permission to reprint as amended. Chapter 6, "How the Family Gap Undercuts Western Freedom" is adapted with permission from an essay that appeared in the *Spectator World* on December 30, 2020; appreciation to editor Dominic Green for his consideration. Chapter 8, "The Doomed Experiment of Christianity Lite", is adapted from "Assisted

Religious Suicide", chapter 6 in my 2013 book, *How the West Really Lost God*; thanks to Templeton Press for reprint permission. "Assisted Religious Suicide" was adapted in turn with permission from *First Things* and based on my 2010 essay "Christianity Lite". The appendix, "The Meanings of *Dobbs*", reprinted here with permission, first appeared in *National Review* as "What the Nurses Knew".

Special thanks to another friend, George Weigel, and to the faculty and students of the Tertio Millennio Seminar in Cracow, Poland. Some of the ideas in this book began as talks given there, especially chapter 9, "What Really Causes Secularization?".

The dynamic Catholic Information Center in Washington, D.C., where I hold the Panula Chair in Christian Culture, continues to build the counterculture thanks to Mitchell Boersma, Emma Boyle, Rosemary Eldridge, Cindy Searcy, Angelica Tom, and Fr. Charles Trullols. So do other friends and colleagues whose conversations have improved these pages, among them Ryan T. Anderson, Susan Arellano, Jonathan and Paige Bronitsky, J.D. Flynn, Stanley Kurtz, Fr. Dominic Legge, Fr. Thomas Joseph White, and Kathryn Jean Lopez, to whom this book is dedicated with admiration.

A salute to Benjamin Ranieri, who keeps my online and other work running on time with verve. I am grateful as well to the indispensable Ignatius Press. Neither *Adam and Eve* installment would have existed without the encouragement and leadership of Mark Brumley and Fr. Joseph Fessio, S.J., and the dedication of Vivian Dudro, Eva Muntean, and the rest of the team.

My husband and intellectual companion of several decades, Nicholas Eberstadt, gracefully puts up with the inconvenience of the writing habit, as do our children. May this second and last installment of *Adam and Eve* suggest new directions for writers to come.

APPENDIX

The Meanings of *Dobbs*

Like most adults today, I barely remember life before *Roe v. Wade*. But I do recall the flashbulb moment when the new world order hit home. One night in 1973, my mother returned from work with something shiny on the collar of her starched white uniform: a silver pin representing two tiny feet. She would wear it at the local hospital from then on, she explained, and so would some of the other nurses. The pins signaled their refusal to participate in abortion—a word I heard that night for the first time.

This was not an association of Catholics. These were nurses, period: medical professionals in a small-city hospital in upstate New York. They knew from their shifts in labor and maternity wards that what grew within a pregnant woman was no mere "clump of cells". Long before the sonogram would settle the question forever, nurses and doctors and midwives and others experienced in handling pregnancy and birth *knew*.

It would take a massive campaign of indoctrination by the country's most elite institutions, and staggering complicity, to try to obliterate that knowledge. Courts and universities, medical schools and prestige journalism, Hollywood and the arts, trend-setters and jet-setters all thronged to the challenge. It would take culture-wide mendacity of a most vigorous and self-interested kind to replace what the nurses knew with one bold lie after another: *Violence toward the unborn is a human right. Mothers and children are natural enemies. Career comes first. My body, my choice.*

Given the sheer scale of that reeducation project, it's no wonder that so many came to believe in rot. As the decades ground on, and the thrown-away piled up, and the hearts and minds pledged to their defense remained mostly outside once-polite society, more and more younger Americans came to hear nothing *but* the gospel according to *Roe*. One by one, their leaders bent before the idol of convenience. So, too, did plenty of their parents, at times even their churches. It fell to self-dealing hucksters like Hugh Hefner to seize the cultural initiative, normalizing the notion that one sophisticated solution to a problem is to kill it.

This brings us to the first extralegal meaning of the *Dobbs* decision: the generations schooled by *Roe* were duped, bigtime, beginning with that majority opinion. The law, as is famously repeated, is a teacher. *Roe* taught scientism, bowdlerized history, and naked will harnessed to faulty logic. *Dobbs*, by extraordinary contrast, teaches constitutional law and history with rigorous, uncompromising reason. The decision says, in effect, "This court and this country took a major wrong turn almost fifty years ago." From now on, the generations deceived by *Roe* can understand this deception for what it was: the court's fault, not theirs.

Yes, a clamorous minority clings bitterly to yesterday's license. In some states, abortion will continue as before— maybe even increase. Corporations broadcast that they will go to great lengths to hold on to their female employees: subsidized abortion, subsidized egg-freezing, and whatever else it takes to make a company woman be more like a man. Even so, pro-choice advocates must now do what they have not had to do for half a century: make their case in the public square. The clarifications will add more transparency to discussions to come, hence are another change for the better.

A second meaning of *Dobbs* is equally bracing. If it has turned out that, under the aegis of the Constitution, abortion on demand requires a second look, then related second looks at today's American experiment might also be in order. These include not only scrutiny of other cases involving substantive due process, as recommended in Justice Clarence Thomas' concurrence. We are also overdue for new critical thinking about society at large after *Roe*, entailing plain English about what the post-1960s social revolutions wrought.

For God's sake, look at where we've been. Sixty-three million abortions since 1973. Sixty-three million human beings prevented from growing into babies and toddlers, teenagers and adults; filling playgrounds, working and marrying, comforting aged parents; enriching the lives of siblings and cousins and friends; enjoying children of their own; staving off by their very existence the ravages of that singularly lethal curse of the age of *Roe*, loneliness.

Look at where we are now—the vaunted "freer", "better" world, in whose name *Roe*'s toll has been committed. It careens toward entropy. During the last few years, American life expectancy has fallen for the first time in our history. Drugs that anesthetize life and conscience course down Main Street. Deprived of a circle of caring people in their lives, for reasons that include nonstop abortion, some among us display the pathologies observed by psychologist Harry Harlow in socially isolated animals, mentioned in chapter 4: aggression and dysfunction. Untethered from their own, they are in free fall.

The clinical varieties of what used to be called "madness" keep rising, especially among the young. And now the feral offspring of a feral era pour unprecedented violence into the streets. Practically to a man, these demented souls share interrupted family trees—another blight that abortion on demand, with its millions of human subtractions, helped to make possible. Barbarism toward small things breeds barbarism toward bigger ones. Who can doubt that the wanton devaluation of nurture enshrined by *Roe* and *Casey* bears some of the unassigned blame here?

Third, *Dobbs* spells vindication of an epochal kind to millions who never expected to see it: those in the pro-life movement. Those priests and nuns, grannies and parents, children and teenagers; those people from all over with their strollers and walkers and wheelchairs; those countercultural doctors and nurses; those penitents and refugees from the sexual revolution; those Americans of every hue and place who have made this fellowship the most small-*c* catholic association in the United States. Every foot soldier now knows in his heart something hitherto accepted in blind faith: the sacrifices were worth it—all of them.

Every last pair of ice-crusted sneakers and socks, marching down the National Mall in frigid January. Every tedious, long trip made for the Cause by anyone, anywhere. Every prayer for the innocent, and for their parents too, lobbed blindly into the cosmos. Every diaper and dime sent to emergency pregnancy centers. Every word uttered or written on behalf of the defenseless. Every sleepless night or waking hour spent taking care of a baby, waiting for a tardy teenager, arranging for an adoption, sitting with a woman in labor, dropping off meals to new families. All of those unbidden acts, seen or unseen, *counted*, and so did every silver pin representing tiny feet.

Dobbs also yields a fourth kind of meaning, this one for politics. In the battles between those who believe the United States to be irredeemable without radical new arrangements and those who do not, a gale wind of momentum has just been sent the latter's way. Hamilton,

Madison, and Jay came through. The federalism that remains one of the wonders of the political world came through. It came through in a way that many since *Roe* had despaired of ever happening again.

Just as *Roe* did before it, that last lesson will race beyond America's statehouses to courts and parliaments around the globe. For years, countries grounded in the same civilization have wearied of their traditionalist pasts and longed for a seat at the Western cool-kid table. A number have lately deep-sixed earlier national laws that proscribed and limited abortion. Now the most prominent court in the world has declared that the law need not rubber-stamp the destruction of the unborn after all. True, recrimination from abroad thunders on—for now. But the claim that legalizing abortion puts a nation in history's swankest corner has been undercut. Without doubt, the second thoughts sparked by *Dobbs* will not be confined to U.S. borders.

Fifth, as has been said truthfully and ad infinitum since the leak of the draft opinion in May, *Dobbs* means that the pro-life movement must pivot to accommodate new work—more checks to be written; more pro bono legal help; more therapy for fragile families; more roofs to shelter innocent heads; more adoption options; more attention to foster care; more time spent in prisons and other places, helping absent and estranged fathers become fathers. In a word, more love.

It also suggests room for initiatives on another side of the ledger: deterrence. Thanks to *Roe*, for a very long time, men with the worst intentions have enjoyed carte blanche to behave heartlessly. That cultural permission now looks shakier than it has in fifty years. Just for starters, in the name of renewed compassion for women, how about doubling the penalties for possession of date-rape drugs and imposing mandatory sentences for their use? And toughening up paternity and child-support laws in every state? And taking a closer look at a commercial surrogacy industry that treats mothers like domesticated animals and babies like high-end consumer choices? For that matter, if America is really more serious than ever about reducing the risks of unexpected pregnancies, how about finally regulating today's chief teacher of brutality toward women: internet pornography?

The long national rave inaugurated by *Roe v. Wade* is over. Its run has been prodigious. Just about every adult now alive checked in on that party somewhere. But what the forces behind *Roe* would never acknowledge, and the forces behind *Dobbs* do, is what that experiment finally proved. There is a floor. There is a level beneath which men and women cannot sink in the name of autonomy without crashing through to a pit. And thanks to the Supreme Court, the United States is now lifted from the depths once more. This is not just a good thing but a great one, to be celebrated and memorialized and passed down with pride like all liberations from bondage, however partial.

So bring on the post-*Dobbs* future. Let voters in every state weigh a framed sonogram photo against a handmaid costume. Let everyone who learned the truths of *Roe*'s legacy the hard way now forgive, including themselves, and move on. Let the Zoomers and Millennials and other Americans shortchanged by family and community collapse come to know the truth: life is good. New life is grand. Let the babies of tomorrow do what babies do, what Americans scarred by *Roe* missed out on: humanize the people around them. And may the continuing, manifestly loving work of the pro-life movement come to soften the hearts of opponents and rekindle something that so many after 1973 thought all but extinguished by law: mercy. Mercy.

INDEX